has been learned, all that life has given, all happiness. Here one discovers the power of a mother's and daughter's love that kept both alive while thousands around them perished. Here one rediscovers the power of each survivor's memoirs to shock with images and perspectives no similar account provides.

"This book is a monument to the enduring qualities of the human spirit and a sober reminder of man's capacity for evil. Its pages will move readers as few books can. It teaches those essential lessons of history that must be learned by today's youth if the twenty-first century is to be less malignant than the century Shari and Magda experienced."

> **F. Jeffrey Platt**
> **Professor of History**
> **Northern Arizona University**
> **Flagstaff, Arizona**

Shirley Lebovitz and daughter Magda Willinger with love

"The Enduring Spirit *dramatically narrates the odyssey of two survivors from the Polish death camp at Auschwitz to their native land. In a world gone mad in wanton killing and destruction, this book limns a remarkable study in the psychology of survival. Its pages describe how these two Jewish women survive the horrors of the Holocaust and return home undaunted in spirit but scarred for life emotionally.*

"Pervading this book is the somewhat muted message of an inspired Jewish Christian, who wrote that 'God is love and he who dwells in love, dwells in God and God in him.' (1 John 4:16)."

                Rev. Ernest F. Latko, O.F.M., S.T.D. Ph.D.
                Adjunct Instructor of World Religions
                    and Ethics
                Kankakee Community College
                Kankakee, Illinois

"I am pleased to endorse your efforts as a meaningful work in the area of Holocaust studies.

"As is known by all of us, it is important to continue to relate the horrors of that event, 'lest we forget,' so that it may never happen again."

                Fife Symington
                Governor, State of Arizona

"Simply told from the heart, this is a true and deeply moving tale of the love a mother and daughter, each determined to save the other from incred-

ible dangers and adventures. In spite of the heartbreaking elements, there is a 'sweetness' in the story. The reader experiences a new respect for the basic dignity and the enduring spirit of man. This story is especially important now when the world is again threatened by neo-Nazism and the chilling philosophy of racial cleansing.

"It is impossible to put the book down; a real page-turner."

          Dorothy Pickelner
          Book Reviewer
          Phoenix Book Club
          Phoenix, Arizona

"I have always found it difficult to express my feelings after reading of the unbelievable and inhumane events that took place in Europe up to and during World War II. Only those who were the victims will ever know and understand. The Enduring Spirit *affected me differently than all other accounts I have read on the Holocaust. I was moved to understand this dark time in our world as more than a historical event, but a personal tragedy that affected individual lives and families forever.*

"As a pastor, I urge Christians to read this book and from this personal account understand that we cannot allow this tragedy to ever happen again."

          Pastor George Morrison
          Faith Bible Chapel
          Arvada, Colorado

THE
ENDURING
SPIRIT

THE ENDURING SPIRIT

THE INSPIRING TRUE STORY OF A HOLOCAUST SURVIVOR

BY SHIRLEY LEBOVITZ

In Collaboration With Greta Bishop

Translated From the Hungarian
by Magda Willinger

Gildith Press

Copyright © 1993 Shirley Lebovitz

All rights reserved. Except for use in a review, the reproduction or use of work in any form by any electronic, mechanical or other means now known or invented hereafter, including xerography, photocopying, recording, information storage and retrieval systems, is forbidden without the written permission of the publisher.

Manufactured in the United States of America. This edition published by Gildith Press, P.O. Box 22102, Phoenix AZ 85028.

First Printing April 1993

Second Printing June 1995

Third Printing March 1998

10 9 8 7 6 5 4 3 2 1

Library of Congress Catalog Card Number 93-77469

Lebovitz, Shirley
The enduring spirit, the inspiring true story of a holocaust survivor.
1. Jews—Hungary—persecutions. 2. Jews—Czechoslovakia—persecutions. 3. Holocaust, Jewish (1939-1945)—Personal narratives. 4. World War, 1939-1945. 5. Hungary—Ethnic relations. 6. Czechoslovakia—Ethnic relations. I. Title.

1993   817.54   93-77469

ISBN 0-9635993-0-5

Printed in the United States by Morris Publishing

**LOVINGLY DEDICATED TO
THE MEMORY OF**

Gitl Klein, mother

David Klein, brother

Blanche Klein, sister

Lenke Klein, sister-in-law

Pearl Klein, niece

Josef Klein, nephew

Solomon Weisberger, husband

Veronica Weisberger, daughter

Lillian Weisberger, daughter

Bertha Weisberger, mother-in-law

Esther Weisberger, sister-in-law

Margaret Kraus, sister-in-law

TABLE OF CONTENTS

Prologue	xiii
Chapter 1	17
Chapter 2	33
Chapter 3	56
Chapter 4	89
Chapter 5	116
Chapter 6	144
Chapter 7	173
Chapter 8	233
Chapter 9	275
Epilogue	303
Acknowledgments	311

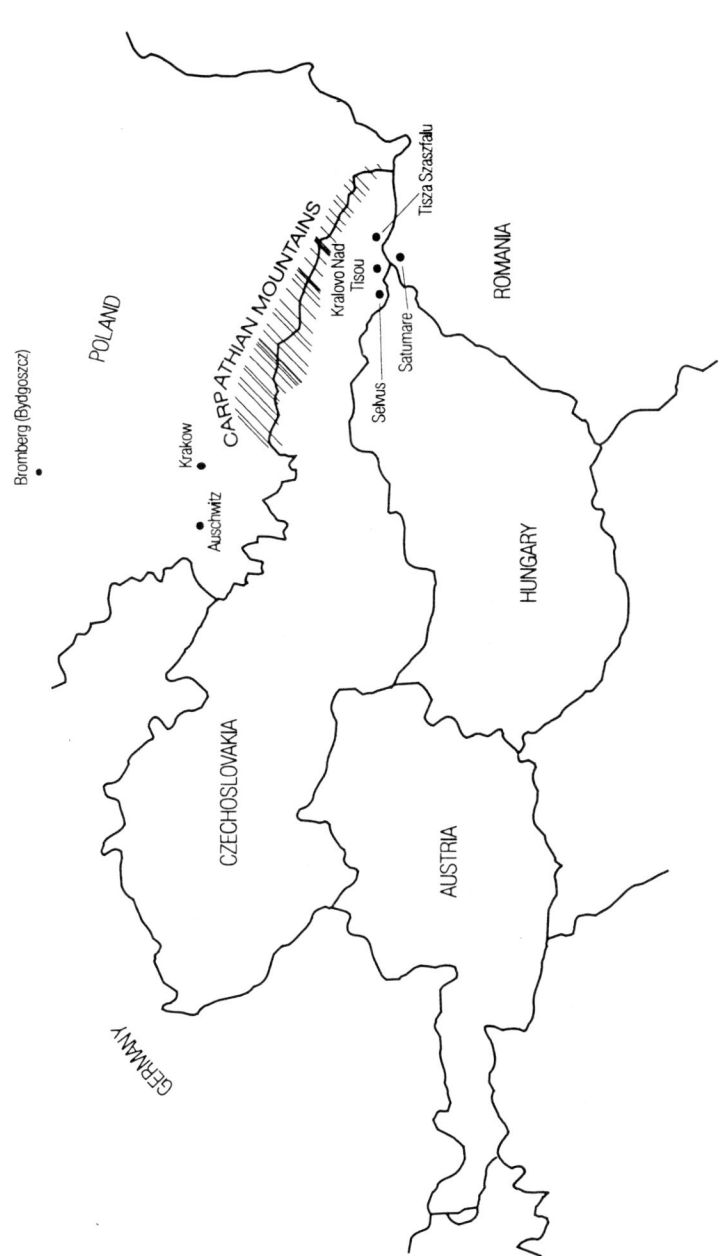

PROLOGUE

The Republic of Czechoslovakia, which Hitler was determined to destroy, was the creation of the peace treaties after World War I. Carved out of the Hapsburg Empire, which in the sixteenth century had acquired the ancient Kingdom of Bohemia and Moravia as well as Slovakia and Ruthenia, Jews and Gypsies, Czechoslovakia developed during the years that followed its founding in 1918 into the most democratic, progressive, enlightened and prosperous state in Central Europe. Within the country lived one million Hungarians, half a million Ruthenians and three and a quarter million Sudeten Germans.

Compared to minorities in most other countries, including America, those in Czechoslovakia lived a rewarding life. They enjoyed full democratic and civil rights—including the right to vote—and were given, to some degree, their own schools and permitted to maintain their own cultural institutions. Leaders of the minority political parties often served as ministers in the central government.

Geographically speaking, the Czechlosovakian position in Europe was that of a small nation providing a strategically important border between the East and the West. The Czechs faced the Germans on three sides, which accounts for the strong impact of Western influence upon this tiny country, and its recurrent confrontations with the Germans.

In 1933, when Hitler became Chancellor, National Socialism struck the Sudeten Germans. In that year, the Sudeten German Party (S.D.P.) was formed under the leadership of a mild-mannered gymnastics teacher, Konrad Henlein. By 1935, the party was being secretly subsidized by the German Foreign Office, and Hitler's own view of the Czechs had become no less prejudicial than those of the Sudeten German extremists.

After approximately five years of army rule, it was decided that the leader of the Sudeten Germans would take over the government, suppressing all independent Czech political and cultural institutions, assimilating the entire population and causing this territory to become basically German in character.

In 1938-39, Czechoslovakia's place in history

would be determined by circumstances beyond her control. Her interests were opposed to those of Berlin, but her destiny was irrevocably interwoven with that of Nazi Germany.

In the winter of 1939, Hitler made his decision to crush Prague and prepare for the liquidation of Czechoslovakia. The Sudeten Germans began to foment new manifestations, organizing anti-Czech and anti-Jewish demonstrations in all the Czech cities with a German element. Many Jews, though not yet suffering any serious persecution, encountered discrimination in public employment and professions. There were some minor skirmishes in Prague and Brno, but even so, it was difficult to rouse violence among the Czechs. As a whole, these were a middle-class people owing their greatest achievements to industrious and peaceful work rather than to the use of arms. Nonetheless, Berlin set off a violent press and radio campaign, and this propaganda machine worked full force to protest alleged persecution of Sudeten Germans. Hitler secretly offered a free hand to Hungary in Ruthenia, both he and his foreign minister, von Ribbentrop, urging Hungary to press for their share of the spoils. Hungary did not need much German prodding; it was eager to satisfy its greedy appetite, and so became a willing accomplice to Nazi Germany's imperialistic policies.

While the leaders of these countries plotted and pushed, hundreds of thousands of Eastern European citizens continued their work-a-day lives, unaware that, as pawns in a ruthless play for power, their lives were about to change forever.

1

Prior to Hungary's invasion of the Carpathian Ukraine (Ruthenia), our family resided in the picturesque little community of Kralovo Nad Tisza, bounded by the Carpathian Mountains, a range extending through northern Slovakia, beginning at the Danube. The Carpathian Ukraine at that time was called Pod Karpatska Rus by the Czechs and Ruthenia by the English, and was populated primarily by Hungarians, Ruthenians, Czechs, Gypsies and Jews. The beauty of this particular area rivaled any Alpine landscape and encouraged such popular activities as mountain climbing, swimming in the Tisza River and the more leisurely pastime of watching barges float by with their loads of logs for the lumber mills.

During twenty years of Czech rule, we existed in a basically Democratic society and prospered in our daily affairs according to the free enterprise system. We were known to our friends and neighbors as the Solomon Weisbergers, the parents of two daughters, Magda and Veronica, and the proprietors of a local grocery store and butcher shop. As Jews, we openly practiced our faith and took pride in our accomplishments as did others who functioned as local shoemakers, cabinetmakers, tailors, butchers and village innkeepers. It was a pleasant, simple life and since the population of Kralovo Nad Tisza was only about 6,000, we were not encroached upon by the pressures and vanities of big city life.

But with Hungary's invasion in 1939, all this would change. Hungary, in coalition with Germany, brought an abrupt end to the Democratic freedoms we had always enjoyed, and with that began the nightmare that would plunge our lives into total chaos.

Although there were those who had anticipated the invasion, we were not, for the most part, prepared or even mindful of what was to befall us. Prior to the onset of these horrendous events, my most anxious thoughts concerned themselves with trivial everyday occurrences. For example, I was not above becoming dismayed at a certain overzealous compassion my husband Solomon frequently demonstrated in trading with the local Gypsies. They would come into our store to buy necessary staples and had an artful knack for talking Sol into letting them charge their purchases.

It was impossible to convince him that they had no actual intention of paying their debts. He always believed they were merely down on their luck, a temporary condition that now and again plagued us all.

"You are a hopeless optimist," I would tell him in our native Hungarian, a futile observation at best since he always preferred to accept it as a compliment.

But since this was the worst that could be said about Sol, his faults were an easy burden to bear. He was in all respects a fine man, a devoted husband and father, and the kindest human being I had ever known.

His children adored him. At the time, Magda was eleven, and Veronica only three. They followed him about at a respectful distance, waiting for the cherished smile or gentle ruffling of the hair that always reinforced their feelings of being loved. If Sol would have preferred to have a boy in the family, he never gave any indication of it. He treated the girls as if they were the sunlight in his life, and in the way they sparkled and danced before him, it was obvious that this was so.

Still, with a twinge of something yet undefinable, we sensed that the world was changing. Periodically, the girls would appear before us, distressed and in tears and, after a few moments, we would come to understand the nature of their anguish.

"What's a dirty Jew, Mama? Why do people call us that when we bathe as often as they do?"

Having posed this difficult question, Magda would run from the room, not waiting for an answer. Perhaps she feared what I might say, or somehow sensed the futility of her question.

In time, anti-Semitic remarks became more commonplace. "Go back to Palestine!" total strangers would sneeringly suggest as we walked along the streets.

In the schools, the Jewish children were subjected to anti-Semitic songs, and eventually, were forced to sing along.

I watched my own children become fretful and withdrawn, immersed in a guilt that had no name. Their anguished glances followed us as we moved about, attempting to go on with our lives as if none of this were happening, as if these events did not have some major underlying significance too ominous to consider.

But there was no denying the alarming reports being transmitted by Radio Prague, broadcasts that repeatedly cautioned against resisting the German army and spoke of alleged excesses against ethnic minorities.

Later, we would learn that the tone of these bewildering broadcasts had been set by Hitler's fateful meeting with the Czechoslovakian president, Emil Hacha. At that meeting, the Fuehrer pressured Hacha into signing a declaration that officially placed the fate of Czechoslovakia and its people in the hands of the German Reich. And while a peaceful occupation was a foregone conclusion, Hacha telephoned Prague and ordered that there be no resistance to invading troops, for he still feared a wholesale slaughter.

In our own little part of this turbulent country, we became increasingly confused and fearful of the Nazis' intentions, as reflected in the actions of those volatile, unpredictable Hungarians who chose to become allied with them.

The Hungarians were eager to obtain Ruthenia, which had also been offered to the Ukranians. Under a brief period of Ukranian rule, we saw the formation of a ragtag army, comprised of such unlikely specimens as our own local woodchopper. We had always thought of him as a kind and gentle soul who went from house to house, offering to chop our wood. We always gave him what work we could, enjoying his regular visits and shy, almost timid ways. And then, one morning, we awoke to see this same woodchopper striding through town in a makeshift uniform with a rifle on his shoulder. He took no notice of us that day, staring straight ahead and walking with an air that suggested some higher purpose. The Hungarians were much better organized and equipped, however, and the Ukranian rule was short-lived. In the end, the Hungarians lined up this motley army along the banks of the Tisza River and shot them all. The dead bodies floating in the water contaminated not only the river but the fish as well, since they ingested all manner of foreign substances, including jewelry and pocket watches which they found on the dead men.

Meanwhile, our lives continued, although not as prosperously as before. When our businesses began to suffer, we forced ourselves to believe we were merely involved in a temporary downward trend. And while we did our best to see ourselves through this so-called recessionary period, dark forces were at work which would eventually make the Jews and Slavic peoples the *Untermenschen*, subhumans whom Hitler would declare unfit to live. Still, a goodly number of them would be delivered to the Gestapo to be placed in the service of the Reich for the betterment of the German people. A designated number were forced to toil in the mines or work in some agricultural capacity, while others did what they could to promote the war effort. This practice would eventually lead to the formation of Hungarian forced labor camps, such as the one my husband was assigned to for eight to ten months each year. For twenty cents a day, he helped dig trenches and build roads and bridges for the military along the front lines.

Each time he returned to us, we saw we had lost something more of the man we had always loved and depended upon. It amounted to a gradual erosion of the spirit, the transformation of a proud, upstanding individual into a sickly, stoop-shouldered figure in ragged clothes.

The children no longer skipped about and joked with him. Sensing his rawboned fatigue, they did not try to entice him into their games. With increasing frequency, they withdrew from his short temper and racking cough, and tried to adjust to this new stranger in the house.

"I am sorry," he would say to me again and again. "I should do more things with the children. We have so little time together. Perhaps tomorrow will be better. A good night's sleep and some decent food will help."

"You have nothing to apologize for," I always insisted, not caring for this new apologetic quality in him. It demeaned him in some way and I did not care to be a witness to that. Many Jewish businesses had lost their license to operate by now. At every turn, we saw another tobacco shop, liquor store or restaurant shut its doors for the last time. In my own case, I found that I could not efficiently operate two businesses on my own and reluctantly sacrificed the butcher shop in order to be able to salvage the grocery store.

While Sol was away, I sent packages to the labor camp, including what small provisions I could gather together to make his life a little easier. We had now begun to live under truly fretful conditions, and at times, the responsibilities of two small children and a business seemed more than I could manage.

Each time that Sol would leave us, I would see him off with a mounting sense of panic. I knew that with each parting, we were flirting with the possibility of a permanent separation. When I would return to the house—alone—it always seemed dark inside, even at midday.

The children did not understand why their father was compelled to return to a place that was visibly breaking his health and spirit, and there was no logical way to explain it to them.

"Will Papa come home again?" they would ask each time, and I always tried to sound confident in my assurances that he would.

And yet, despite long separations, and the hardships to be faced at home, our life continued with some semblance of normalcy.

When nothing is as it should be, one clings to the comforts of routine and habit. The house still needed to be cleaned, the cow still needed to be milked and the children continued to enjoy their role of helping when and where they could.

In the fall, we would force-feed our geese for approximately four weeks since at the end of that time, each bird was capable of yielding up to two quarts of fat, an essential ingredient in many of our daily menus. In addition, highly fatted goose liver was considered a delicacy, a gourmet's delight when properly prepared. Even today, it remains a vital ingredient in many Jewish recipes that have earned their place as old family favorites.

The procedure for force-feeding the geese was to straddle each bird and push the grain down its gullet. While I found this practice somewhat distasteful, the girls considered it great sport, particularly if the bird was inclined to buck or run. At that point, they would fight for control and ultimate mastery, much as a rodeo cowboy might, and when the chore was done, they were as dust-covered and disheveled as any bronco rider on the range.

In 1942, our third daughter, Lillian, was born. At the beginning of that year, Hitler had suffered devastating losses after he refused to let the German armies in Russia retreat in time. The winter fighting had exacted a terrible toll, and it appeared possible that the Fuehrer's fanatical determination to advance his forces and gain absolute power might be his undoing.

In retrospect, it seems senselessly apathetic on our part to have continued to believe that some deterrent to Hitler would occur in time to prevent the Holocaust. Still, it seemed to us that the world would not allow the continued advancement of a man or political regime of such demonical magnitude, and certainly, some word of caution for the future exists in these misjudgments of the past. For while we continued to trust and to hope, the Jews were subjected to large-scale dismissals from government jobs. Jewish-owned real estate was confiscated, the practice of intermarriage was prohibited and heavy taxation was placed upon our few remaining assets. In time, these measures would leave the Jewish people impoverished and totally inconsequential except to the extent that they could continue to serve the Reich.

Slovakian officials had already begun to negotiate with the Germans for removal of the Jews and, when the Germans demanded 20,000 additional workers from Slovakia, 20,000 Slovak Jews ranging in age from sixteen to thirty-five were immediately supplied. It cannot be firmly established how much the Slovak government actually knew about the ultimate fate of the Jews, although by July 1942, rumors of "death camps" had already begun circulating. There was already even talk that the more unfortunate among us could be expected to be "boiled into soap."

Ironically, a personal problem of my own just then concerned the matter of soap. Having been forced to liquidate my assets in the grocery store, I suffered considerable losses and knew at once that the money I had realized from this forced sale would not last very long.

For a brief period, I gave in to overpowering waves of panic and distress. I was barely able to function during the day because I was not able to sleep at night. My mother-in-law, Bertha, who lived only one block away, began visiting daily. She moved with quiet grace through the rooms, seeing to it that the household ran smoothly and that the children were attended to. She tried to preoccupy them in subtle ways when they were inclined to make demands upon me. From a large overstuffed chair in a corner of the living room, she eyed me skeptically over the quick, clicking movement of her knitting needles. I sensed that she feared I would break under the strain of mounting responsibilities and pressures. I vowed to reinforce her confidence in me, even as I sought to reinforce my own. After all, there were those who depended upon me. For their sakes, if not my own, I would have to take some positive action and attempt to make the best of things.

"I have to leave," I abruptly told her one day. "There is someone I must see across the border. If you would stay with the children until I return, I think we will all be the better for it."

Bertha pressed me for additional information but I told her nothing more. In all honesty, I had little faith in the success of the scheme I was plotting, but it was worth a try, because it could mean some extra money in the house.

Since the borders were still open, I journeyed without difficulty to Halmi, Romania, to visit a soap manufacturer by the name of Joseph Weis. This trip was prompted by a growing scarcity of laundry soap and the persistence of my previous customers who continued to approach me in an attempt to uncover some available source.

"Please! I no longer have the store," I would constantly remind them. "There is nothing I can do for you."

"But you must know where soap can be obtained. You had suppliers who brought you what you wanted. You know these people. There must be a way."

Yes, it seemed indeed that there must be a way. And so, in my best dress and with a nice piece of luggage, I journeyed by train to Halmi and then rode a bus to Weis's house.

As I knocked on his door, I discovered that my knees were knocking as well. I had had two hours to rehearse what I would say to Joseph Weis, but now, as his wife opened the door and admitted me, I found I could not remember a word. I was led to the kitchen where Weis sat at the table, eating a large bowl of soup and some crackers.

"This is Mrs. Solomon Weisberger," Weis's wife explained. "She once had a grocery store and butcher shop in Kralovo Nad Tisza. She says she has some business with you."

Joseph Weis waved his arm expansively, indicating that I should be seated. As he continued to eat his soup, his wife brought me some tea and a small snack, and then politely retreated so that Weis and I might speak alone.

I quickly explained my purpose in coming. Although my words were somewhat hesitant and awkward, I managed to convey my message.

"I do not understand, Frau Weisberger," I was disappointed to hear Joseph Weis say. "You appear to be confused about certain things. What has led you to believe that I make soap?"

"Please, Mr. Weis, I know it is true. And I promise you that I would never jeopardize our association or your personal safety through any reckless acts of my own."

"It is a risky business all the same...." Weis mumbled under his breath, and then began shaking his head impatiently when he saw that I meant to persuade him further. "These are treacherous, evil times, Frau Weisberger. You must not ask what you are asking."

"It is not for myself that I ask. I agree with you that these are evil times. It is a time when children are allowed to go hungry and to do without things essential to their health and well-being. Our family cannot last long on what I was forced to take for the store. I have turned the matter around in my mind with endless repetition. I must do what I can, and the source who referred me to you promised that I could rely upon your kindness and understanding."

"What source is that?" Weis asked sharply, and when I mentioned the name, his face slowly relaxed. "I see," he said quietly, and continued to break crackers into his soup until the interminable silence began to grate on my nerves. "Very well," he said at last. "I will help you." And then, with a quick gesture toward my suitcase, he told me to follow him.

On the trip home, I cradled the suitcase in my lap like a beloved child, knowing that if its contents were discovered, my troubles would just be beginning. But if I managed to arrive home safely, some immediate problems would be solved.

Providence was on my side that day and for some days thereafter. I continued along in the business of black marketing soap for a tidy profit until someone reported me to the Hungarian Zandars, an organized police force sporting green uniforms and high hats with fancy feathers. Their regional, quaint appearance was sharply offset by the rifles, bayonets and swords they wielded. Brandishing all of these weapons, they appeared at my home one morning and systematically ransacked it. Whatever soap and money they found, they confiscated. They then took me to the station house, interrogating me all the way.

"Where did you get the soap?"

"I bought it in Halmi on the open market."

"From whom?"

"A local merchant. I don't know his name."

"You are lying."

"I haven't any reason to lie."

"You have *every* reason to lie, you cheap Jewish slut. We'll get to the bottom of this."

In that moment, an icy dagger of fear plunged itself through my heart. I kept wanting to remind them that we were all Hungarian, that the Nazi Regime should not lessen our kinship, although it was clear it had.

I was interrogated for hours by the Hungarian Zandars, wondering at the strange new violence in these men. While I would never have associated them with such tactics, they began to hit me with the butts of their rifles. The shock of the first blow enveloped me in an agonizing wave of pain.

"Now you will tell us what we want to know," one of them insisted again with a chilling calm.

"I don't know what it is you want of me."

"The *truth*!" one of the Zandars shouted, and swung at me again with all his force.

The sound of one particular blow had an ominous tone. Each breath was sudden fire and the room began to spin, and I felt certain he had cracked my ribs.

"Don't waste our time," one of the officers sneered. "We know all about you. You have been under surveillance for months."

I looked into his glacier-blue eyes and decided he was lying. My chest was aching and the bruises on my face had begun to bleed. Feeling weak and beaten, I mustered what remaining strength I had and continued to profess my innocence. If my captors were convinced, they gave no outward indication of it, although they eventually allowed me to leave.

When I arrived home, I was so preoccupied with my good fortune at having escaped some crueler fate that I gave no thought to my actual appearance. But once I had entered the house, I realized the truth in the stricken looks of my children and mother-in-law. As they cried out in horror, I quickly moved to a hall mirror and examined the ugly cuts, welts and bruises on my face and limbs. Only then did the stark reality of the situation come home to me.

"It isn't as bad as it seems," I told them in a voice that trembled unconvincingly, and for a time, we all sat together and cried over the horrible state of the world.

"You cannot continue the business with the soap, Shari," my mother-in-law warned, perhaps already sensing my determination to continue with my black market activities.

"Don't concern yourself about that," I told her defiantly. "It can be managed. I will simply have to be more cautious in my methods."

"Shari, they will ki—" she started, but then remembered the children in the room.

After that, she said nothing more, but her eyes continued to plead with me as she dressed my wounds and assured the girls that their mother was not seriously hurt.

After a few days, I began to suspect that she might be right. Once the pain in my rib cage had subsided, I gave no further thought to the possibility of broken bones.

Since there were no telephones available except for those at the post office, the police station and the bank, people could only deal with me by coming to the house. Each time there was a knock on the door, my heart would stop until I realized that it was only one of my customers and not the Zandars returning to arrest me again.

It was all a dreadful business, but I consoled myself with the thought that we were decent, honorable business people, that we had never before defied the law, and that we only did so now because it was necessary to our survival and because the law was unjust.

2

The family into which I was born resided in the small village of Tisza Szaszfalu, approximately ten kilometers from where I now lived.

Our family name was Klein and its members included an older sister and brother, Sarah and David, younger sisters Pearl and Blanche, and the baby of the family, our brother Adolph. It amused me that my sister Pearl had been somewhat embarrassed at Adolph's birth so late in my mother's life, but the reason for this was that my father had made several trips to the United States, and each time, was gone for an extended period of time. Adolph was not born until after my father had made his third journey to America. That trip was the longest, and also his final one.

He had hoped to bring us all to this land of opportunity and worked long and hard to accumulate the necessary funds to do so. He was a butcher by trade and had come to realize that the modest population of our village, which included roughly thirty-five Jewish families, could not support us nearly so well as some of the larger, more flourishing communities in America.

On his third trip there, my sister Sarah accompanied him. Soon after World War I, he wrote a long letter to my mother, insisting that now was the time for the family to make the move. He spoke of sending us the necessary papers, obviously intending for us to come at once.

My mother was visibly alarmed by the thought of this sudden uprooting. In the past, it had all merely been idle chatter, but now the day appeared to be upon us, and we children found her greatly distressed. Being a highly religious person, she feared we would not be allowed to practice our faith in this new country, and so hesitated to make the move.

Meanwhile, my father returned to us, and when he arrived, we found he had approximately four thousand dollars, a veritable fortune in those days. But he vacillated for a time on whether to convert the dollars into crowns. His indecision cost him dearly, for the value of the American dollar began to decline, and finally there were only funds enough to purchase ten acres of farming land and to establish dowries for his daughters, who were rapidly approaching marriageable age. After that, he worked his land until he succumbed to tuberculosis in 1942. While he had always appeared contented with his lot, one can only wonder about such things.

In those days, people accepted poverty and privation on their own terms, paying the price that life demanded, without question or complaint. Throughout my father's long absences, we had all sensed a quiet, dependable strength in our mother. It did not occur to us, and possibly not even to her, that she was ill-equipped to manage alone with four children. The day-to-day struggle must have been overwhelming. While World War I was still under way, my father was not permitted to correspond with us from the United States, nor could he send us money. Throughout these long seven years, my mother operated a small store that stocked rice, sugar, salt, vinegar, kerosene for the lamps and other items people could not produce for themselves. People bartered a great deal in those days, and they would come in with such things as eggs, wheat and corn, which my mother would weigh and then give them a price on. The price she quoted was, in effect, treated as a credit on merchandise in our store.

In addition to the stock we had on hand, we were also taught to make cigarettes and do whatever else we could to make ends meet. It was a difficult life but, since it represented the current average standard of living, we did not feel greatly deprived even though we must have sensed that others had much more. Still, we were not envious, because our affection and support of one another compensated us in many other ways.

My husband's family was much the same, although my mother-in-law, Bertha, was fated to become a widow, and at the start of Hitler's regime, lived with her two daughters, Ethel, a single girl, and Margaret Kraus, a divorcee with two children, Joseph, whom we also called Joska, and Wilma. Bertha operated a small hotel near the railroad station until she lost her license along with the rest of us, but her daughters were dressmakers and secretly pursued this profession to provide for the family.

I do not think that any of us thought of ourselves as having exceptional strength or endurance. Later, after the concentration camps, we would hear ourselves described in this manner, but I know I speak for many when I say that this was not our own feeling on the subject. It is just that certain times and events demand certain things of people, and human resiliency and the desire to survive will emerge and manifest their powers to the extent that they are needed.

In the summer of 1942, we began to be tested in our ability to withstand first one tragedy and then another. By then, my sister Pearl had already met and married a cousin of the family, Louis Stein, who had taken her to America to live. She was fortunate to have escaped the horrendous experiences we would know as a family, for from that point on, our lives would be greatly altered by a series of tragic occurrences.

The first of these involved the induction of my brother Adolph into a labor camp. We learned that he was to report on October 1, 1942, which struck me as altogether incredible. After all, Adolph was the baby of our family, and it did not seem possible that he could already be twenty-one years old. The family had always adored him, granting him the special affection that frequently goes to the youngest child. We felt protective toward him, a trait he heartily encouraged in us when he was a child. Later, he was amused by it, and finally became embarrassed after he had established his own circle of friends, which included any number of attractive young girls. At that point, he hadn't any further use for the mollycoddling of his sisters, but we subjected him to it all the same. He was a handsome blond youth with striking blue eyes and a highly ambitious nature. He hoped to attend a school of commerce to develop the managerial skills necessary to succeed in business. It seemed such a waste to delegate his obvious attributes and vibrant youth to the abysmal task of furthering the Nazi war effort.

On August 24, 1942, Adolph reveled in his last opportunity to be young and carefree on the occasion of a girlfriend's birthday party. On such a warm day, a quick plunge into the cool, sparkling waters of the Tisza River simply could not be resisted.

Adolph was strong and athletic, an excellent

swimmer with a tendency to leave all others behind in any sort of competition. For that reason, none of the partying youngsters paid any attention when he began to cry for help, or when his head disappeared beneath the surface of the water. Twice, then three times it reappeared as his anxious cries continued.

"Louder! Louder, Adolph!" the boys called back tauntingly. "If you would really have us believe that you are drowning, you must attempt to sound more convincing!"

But instead of becoming louder, his cries became weaker—and then, abruptly, ceased.

The sudden, strange silence had an ominous affect on the rest of the group, but they would not allow themselves to be so easily persuaded.

One of the boys pointed to a spot along the shoreline where a tall rock with a wide, flat surface jutted out across the water like a diving board sculptured from stone. "Watch over there!" the boy said. "Adolph will pick that spot to surface. After he's given us all a good scare, he'll appear on that rock. It's his favorite place to sun himself."

As the moments ticked by and Adolph did not appear, the girls became nervous and frightened. The birthday girl ran anxiously up and down the shore, calling out across the water in a voice that trembled with fear and anger. "Adolph, stop this! Your little joke has gone far enough. You're ruining my party with these dreadful pranks, do you hear?"

As time passed, the possibility that Adolph was playing a prank became less certain. Still, it was not unreasonable to assume that he had managed to come ashore at some point beyond their vision and that he was even now, sitting behind a rock or tree, laughing at them.

But as the sun began its gradual decline behind the hills, the youngsters became united in the unspeakable horror of having witnessed a drowning.

"I-It must have been a cramp," one of the boys mumbled in stunned disbelief. "There're some deep places out there—a-and strong currents."

"But he was such a good swimmer!" a girl's high-pitched voice wailed out in protest against the truth. "There wasn't any reason to believe that—oh God, we let him die! We stood by and laughed and actually *let him die!*"

As they all tried to discourage her fit of hysteria, it amounted to discouraging a chain reaction in themselves. They clung to one another, trembling and sobbing quietly, trying to think how this day's events could possibly be recounted in a way that would be understood by Adolph's family. It had all been a mistake, a dreadful miscalculation that could never be undone, but there had not been anything deliberately malicious connected with it. Could that much at least be properly conveyed?

When I first learned of the death of my brother, I reacted as anyone does, questioning the reason for such a senseless tragedy, and the wisdom of a God who permitted such things to happen. It seemed to me that the world had nothing but cruelty and suffering to offer at every turn. Had we not already endured enough without the loss of this precious boy who had viewed the world with such faith and optimism? His personal plans and dreams continued to haunt me as I sent a telegram to my husband in the labor camp so that he might be granted a three-day furlough. Unfortunately, this action resulted in nothing more than a stupid blunder in timing, for by the time my husband arrived home, Adolph had already been buried.

By now, the quality of our life had changed in a way we knew was irreversible. Hitler's conquests had been staggering. Germany and Italy together held most of the northern shore from Spain to Turkey, and the southern shore from Tunisia to within a few miles of the Nile. German troops stood guard from the Norwegian North Cape on the Arctic Ocean to Egypt and, on August 23, 1942, reached the Volga just north of Stalingrad. By the end of August, Hitler was amassing all available forces to launch an attack on the Soviet oil center of Grozny, determined to get his hands on these oil fields.

It seemed to us that whatever he was determined to get his hands on somehow fell into his grasp. As his shadow grew longer and fell across yet another area of the world, we retreated even further into ourselves and reflected upon times that perhaps might never be again.

Throughout the twenty years of Czechoslovakia's Democratic system of government, everyone had always lived in harmony, and there was a peaceful comingling of Hungarians, Ruthenians, Czechs and Jews. The Jewish children attended primarily Czech and Ruthenian schools, and all Jews were allowed to worship freely.

But once the Nazis awakened Hungarian and Ruthenian Fascism with the promise of independence, the Jews could no longer hope to live quietly and inconspicuously as they had always preferred to do.

We were understandably confused and sensitive to the sudden change in the attitudes of the Hungarians and Ruthenians. Anti-Semitism, no longer repressed, was a dreadful thing to experience among those we had always counted as friends.

We began to fear and distrust everyone we knew, and learned to keep to ourselves and function under a blanket of secrecy as if daily survival itself had become a crime against the State.

My soap business faltered and finally had to be discontinued when Mr. Weis could no longer obtain the necessary ingredients. At this point, I vowed I would not again give in to panic. It was a useless and dissipating emotion and, once it passed, matters still had to be resolved.

I looked about for other things to do and learned of a place in Satumare, Romania, where yard goods could be purchased. Such lovely silks and rayons and printed cottons could be resold to be made into ladies garments. It would afford the same risks that the soap business had, but I was used to such risks by now. The same day I conceived of the idea, I spoke with my mother-in-law about it and then immediately prepared for my first trip to Satumare.

A certain ingenuity is born of desperate circumstances. While I had never been given to guile or deception, I became surprisingly good at it. With the yard goods, I devised any number of ways for transporting it from Satumare without detection. In the winter, it was relatively easy. I could wind thirty or forty yards of material around my body and then cover it with a coat. I made the trip monthly and was always able to return home the same day, whereupon I would sell my purchases for a nice profit. Bertha attended to the children while I was gone and maintained something of a nervous vigil at the window, fearing, as always, that my smuggling activities would be discovered and that I would be forced to pay some ugly price for having committed these indiscretions.

As the weather turned warm, Bertha became increasingly tense about the entire situation, pointing out that the yard goods could no longer be concealed under my clothing. She was right, of course, and as summer approached, I fell into the habit of dressing very elegantly, and carrying with me—as a fashionable accessory—my finest piece of luggage. At the time, I was an attractive, blond woman in my mid-thirties, and since I did not look at all Jewish, I was able to get by without arousing suspicion.

On one occasion, as I was boarding the train home with my suitcase full of cotton goods, I was startled to see a member of the Hungarian Zandars Police Force boarding behind me.

"May I help you with your luggage?" he asked politely and, as his hand reached for it, I hesitated only a moment before allowing him to take it. I was certain in my own mind that his chivalry was, in fact, part of some clever confiscation process, but as he gently led me to a vacant seat and helped me settle myself for the journey home, I began to feel that his motives might be sincere.

As he swung his tall, lean body into the seat beside me, he remarked on how heavy the suitcase was.

"Yes, that is the fault of my mother," I explained with a quick, nervous laugh. "Whenever I visit her in Satumare, she never lets me leave until she has packed my suitcase with homemade cookies and cakes for her grandchildren. That is simply her way and I cannot change it, although I have tried, since it is not even good for youngsters to have so many sweet things."

"How many children do you have?" he asked curiously.

"Three daughters," I told him.

"And lovely girls, without a doubt, since their

mother is also quite lovely."

As I thanked him for this compliment, I blushed with flustered embarrassment. I had not yet begun to trust this situation, for it seemed that things were progressing too smoothly. Finally, however, we arrived at my destination and, when I made a move to depart from the train, no effort was made to restrain me. In fact, the officer actually kissed my hand in a very continental fashion and wished me a good day.

"Oh God in Heaven, you were good to me today," I murmured under my breath as I walked up the front steps of our house.

When my mother-in-law asked about my day, I debated whether or not to tell her of my experience, and then decided against it. I knew she would not be consoled by my narrow escape, but would be more inclined to worry about the next time—when things might not go so well.

In the days that followed, life continued along relatively uneventfully. In the normal course of my activities, I made the acquaintance of a Catholic woman who wished to purchase yard goods in fairly large quantities so that she might resell them, just as I was doing. We discussed the level of secrecy that would have to be maintained in our negotiations, and I was careful to instruct her in the best ways to transport the goods. Based on methods I myself was using, I even suggested some hiding places around the house for the money she would earn. Although she was inclined to buy more goods than I felt was safe for her to travel with, I decided that I was becoming too much like my own mother-in-law in constantly fretting over her circumstances. She was certainly as capable of looking after herself as I was, and deserved to be trusted to operate in her own best interests. I decided to give her no further advice or words of warning, especially since I could see that she had begun to resent what she perceived as my interference.

But soon after we had begun trading regularly, this same woman was arrested as she got off the train in her hometown. Under the relentless pressure of interrogation, she was quick to confess where she had purchased her goods. To make things easier on herself, she even told the police what she had paid for the material, and where I was inclined to hide my money.

The next day, two Zandars came to visit me. As I lay in bed suffering the effects of a severe gallbladder attack, they ransacked the entire house, confiscating the goods, and the money I had hidden in a tall chest of drawers.

Then they turned their attentions to me. "Get out of that bed, you dirty Jew bastard!" they ordered. When I insisted I was too ill to comply, they pulled me out and threw me to the floor. As I cowered in a far corner of the room, I watched them tear the mattress and pillows apart, looking for additional money or anything else of value.

I had grown so weak I could barely stand, and as if the symptoms of my illness were not debilitating enough, I was literally paralyzed with fear. As I clung to first one piece of furniture and then another in a vain attempt to cure my trembling, the Zandars quickly approached and roughly tore my hands loose. With nothing to support me, I immediately sank to the floor and listened helplessly as they ordered me to my feet and told me to come along. In the end, I was half-dragged, half-carried along, for the Zandars quickly lost patience with my inability to function as efficiently as they wished.

At the station house, I endured the same abuse I had experienced earlier, but took heart as the door opened and the Police Commissioner, Joseph Szalai, entered the room. Here was an individual who had once been a regular customer in our grocery store, someone who had been allowed to charge his purchases, and who still had a balance owing at the time the store was forced to close.

As I hastened to explain the deplorable manner in which the Zandars had been treating me, he rudely interrupted and commanded that I be silent. Although I could not believe that such things were possible, I saw now that he intended to support the actions of his officers. There was no glimmer of remembrance or even a hint of humanity in his eyes as the verbal browbeating and physical abuse continued. He stood by indifferently as the Zandars labeled me a traitor and a prostitute, and assaulted me with language that was inexcusably vile.

"How can you allow this to continue?" I wailed as the Zandars jerked me about by the hair. "You and I were friends, Joseph Szalai! Have you forgotten?" His answer was to turn his back and stare out the window as the attack upon me became more intensified. There was no hint of compassion in that profile, as rigid as stone, or even any acknowledgment of what was occurring in that room. All in a moment, he had become as militant and ruthless as those he served, as if the past did not exist, or else, did not matter. I found that I could not dismiss our past association as lightly as he, forget a time when we had been friendly and civilized toward one another, as true human beings were intended to be. If I continued to plead with him, perhaps I could ignite some small spark of humanity in this robotized version of a man.

"Please! I am a sick woman, and the mother of three small children. You must let me go!" I cried out in one final bid for compassion.

"Sick, are you?" Szalai sneered. "I don't pity you, Frau Weisberger. You understand the law, and yet you persist in violating it. If you were really concerned about your three children, you would not live as you do. Your troubles are all of your own making. If it were up to me, I would shoot every one of you Jewish bastards today. That is how much I hate your breed. Now, tell us what we want to know!"

His eyes were so cold and unfeeling, his voice

so deadly that I knew I could not count on anything in our past association to work for me now. At long last, I answered all of their questions and, after enduring several more hours of torment, was finally released.

Had the entire world ended in the next moment, I doubt I would have cared, since for me, it already had. No kind of existence was possible without some financial means, and at every turn these sources were being taken away from me.

It occurred to me then that my husband would be returning soon, looking forward to a brief respite from the labor camp and whatever comforts his modest home could provide. At this juncture, those comforts would be meager indeed, because with every passing day we had fewer freedoms and possessions to call our own.

By the time he arrived, I had disguised the remains of my cuts and bruises but feared my cosmetic touches might not pass close inspection.

Still, I need not have worried, for the figure that appeared in our doorway one rainy afternoon had lost the ability to concentrate on such things with any real curiosity or interest.

As Sol slowly lowered his weary body into the nearest chair, I saw how pale and consumptive he had become. His bony shoulders protruded sharply through his ragged coat, and his eyes stared fixedly at a spot on the other side of the room. As the girls tugged gently on his arm, he patted them absentmindedly and rewarded them with a weak smile.

With a sense of mounting panic, I realized that he was incapable of enduring much more of this. He was no longer young enough or strong enough to perform such hard and dangerous work. Many who had worked along the front lines with him had long since died of either disease or starvation, some considerably younger than Sol. The way he had driven and somehow sustained himself was beyond my comprehension. Taking into account the inhuman conditions that had to be endured in a slave labor camp, he could not have been marked for survival. And yet, he had survived.

Although he was obviously undernourished, he picked listlessly at the meal I had prepared for him and, finally, pushed his plate away. "I am sorry," he apologized, humbly and dejectedly. "It is all very good what you have made, Shari. It is only that I am so tired. I believe a little rest would do wonders for my appetite."

I saw the children's faces fall, as they often had in the past. The word "tired" was an unwelcome signal that they must leave their father alone and, after so many months of separation, their childlike enthusiasm was not easily contained. But by now, they understood the rules with a wisdom far beyond their years. Silently, I watched them back away, looking to me for a word on whether to stay or go.

In that moment I felt as if I could no longer

contain my inner anguish. Our lives had been so severely altered by circumstances outside our control that we were rapidly becoming strangers to one another. We coexisted under a constant cloud of hopelessness and despair, wondering how we might have caused these dreadful things to befall us.

And it was not to end there. Soon afterward, we were ordered to prominently display a five-inch yellow star on the left chest side of every garment we wore. To the world, it blatantly identified us as Jews, and the recognition it brought was of the most debasing kind.

Unbeknown to us, the "Final Solution," an irreversible decision aimed at destroying an entire race of people, had already been set into motion.

Perhaps Hitler's party secretary best summed up their long-range intentions when he said:

> The Slavs are to work for us. In so far as we don't need them, they may die. Therefore, compulsory vaccination and German health services are superfluous. The fertility of the Slavs is undesirable. They may use contraceptives or practice abortion—the more the better. Education is dangerous. It is enough if they can count up to 100. . . . Every educated person is a future enemy. Religion we leave

to them as a means of diversion. As for food they won't get any more than is absolutely necessary. We are the masters. We come first.

Propagation of a master race necessitated the need to convince the world that all other nationalities were inferior. The Jews, unfortunately, were considered the least desirable and hence the least worthy of survival.

Evidence that a written "Final Solution" order actually existed was revealed in testimony given at Nuremberg by Dieter Wisliceny, Adolph Eichmann's assistant in Slovakia, Greece and Hungary. Wisliceny recalled the following:

> I was sent to Berlin in July or August 1942 in connection with the status of Jews from Slovakia . . . I was talking to Eichmann in his office in Berlin when he said that on written order of Himmler all Jews were to be exterminated. I requested to be shown the order. He took a file from the safe and showed me a top-secret document with a red border, indicating immediate action. . . . The letter read substantially as follows: 'The Fuehrer has decided that the final solution of the Jewish question is to start immediately. I designate the Chief of the Security Police and S.D. and the Inspector of Concentration Camps as responsi-

ble for the execution of this order. . . . I am to be informed currently as to the execution of this order.

The order was signed by Himmler and was dated some time in April 1942. Eichmann told me that the words 'final solution' meant the biological extermination of the Jewish race, but that for the time being, able-bodied Jews were to be spared and employed in industry to meet current requirements. I was so much impressed with this document which gave Eichmann authority to kill millions of people that I said at the time, 'May God forbid that our enemies should ever do anything similar to the German people.' He replied, 'Don't be sentimental—this is a Fuehrer order.'

I realized at the time that the order was a death warrant for millions of people and that the power to execute this order was in Eichmann's hands subject to approval of Heydrich and later Kaltenbrunner. The program of extermination was already underway and continued until late 1944. . . .

The mass extermination of Jews began in Auschwitz in the summer of 1942. The camp by then was already densely populated. More than 150,000 prisoners and laborers were being guarded by some 3,000 SS men. Throughout the summer, a continuous stream of convoys would deliver victims three or four times daily to subsist for awhile in wretchedly inhuman conditions before being asphyxiated in gas chambers and permanently disposed of in an adjoining crematorium.

As ugly rumors about the possible fate of the Jews began to gain more credibility, my husband received an SOS summons to return at once to the labor camp. Since he was hardly in any condition to go, I thought there must be some mistake about these orders and even suggested as much.

"It is no mistake, Shari," he said despondently. "I must go. You will explain it to the children, yes?"

"No!" I cried out in a moment of violent rage. "You are in no condition to go. They must give you time to rest, to recuperate. Of what use can you be to them the way you are?"

I had not meant to voice my distress at his physical appearance quite so bluntly. The entire time he had been home, I had deliberately avoided this subject, not wishing to make him feel worse by pointing out how truly dreadful he looked. But now, the observation hung in the air between us.

"I must go now."

"I-I only mean—you don't look exactly well, Sol."

"I know how I look," he replied matter-of-factly, as one who had long since accepted a sentence of death.

"I'll go with you to the train," I suggested resignedly, once I'd accepted the fact that there was nothing more that could be done to alter this situation.

"No," he said quietly. "Not this time. I want you to stay here."

"B-But why?"

"It is best," he replied, and before he turned his head away, I saw tears glistening in his eyes.

In a grim kind of silence, we prepared for his departure, but when he moved to go, I once again insisted upon going with him.

"No," he said gently. "There is no reason to go down to the train station and display these wretched yellow stars."

In all the confusion, I had totally forgotten about the stars, but now I remembered and gave some earnest consideration to the extent of his embarrassment at being labeled in this distasteful manner. It was only natural that he would prefer not to be made a spectacle of, particularly in front of his wife, who would also be subjected to the insolent stares and comments of those who did not have to suffer the humiliation of being branded this way.

"I understand," I said then, and let him go, looking after his departing figure until it faded from sight.

It was the last time that I would ever see my beloved Sol. Looking back on that day, I realize now that there had been a fatalistic quality about him. Sensing that he would not return to us, he had wished to remember his family in a warm, familiar setting. It would be the only possession he would be allowed to carry with him to his death.

3

In April 1944, the Jewish Passover was recognized and honored in the traditional way, although there was no air of celebration throughout this holiday week. Only a cloud of oppressive sadness prevailed over all.

On April 16th, we were awakened at an early hour by the town crier, who normally did not pass through our village until noon. I knew instinctively that whatever news he had to offer so early in the day would be highly significant. I quickly found my robe and slippers, and headed for the door.

When I reached our front gate, I was abruptly stopped by a soldier with a rifle.

"Halt!" he commanded. "You are not allowed to pass."

I saw at once that he was quite prepared to

enforce this new rule and so quickly returned to the house, where I opened a window and listened carefully to what the town crier had to say.

"All Jewish people are forbidden to leave their homes!" was his incredible message for the day. "All Jewish people must remain in their homes. You are surrounded by soldiers who will not tolerate any disobedience. Whoever dares to hide or run will be immediately shot!"

As he repeated these words again and again, I tried in vain to make some sense of them. What was being suggested here was that we were prisoners in our own homes, seemingly without any need for further enlightenment. It was a situation to be accepted without question, although such an idea was totally inconceivable to me.

My heart was pounding as I returned to our front yard and began to pace back and forth with a kind of frantic precision. Magda and Veronica had joined me by then, and sensing my mounting panic, quickly dissolved into tears.

"Dear God in Heaven, what crime have we committed to deserve this?" I cried aloud, and saw at once that I had accomplished nothing by this question except to make the children even more distraught. After I had taken them back into the house, I saw from the window that some neighbors, known to us as the Schreiber family, were being forced from their home by two Hungarian Zandars, who herded them through the streets as they clutched a few pitiful belongings. The family's eyes were downcast and their aimless, shuffling walk clearly conveyed a feeling of total hopelessness. Then I saw another family taken, and another, and so it continued throughout the day. It occurred to me that these families were all relatively wealthy Jews, and so attempted to console myself with the thought that my few meager possessions would not be of interest to anyone. But eventually I learned that my lack of financial status did not exempt me from this strange exodus, for late in the afternoon, the Zandars suddenly appeared at my door and ordered me to pack.

"You have ten minutes," I was told. "Take two changes of underwear, and some food. No money or valuables."

Since it was just after Passover, during which we had eaten only matzo rather than bread, I hadn't much food in the house and couldn't think of what to assemble with any real sense of practicality. As I stood there, motionless and mentally numb, one of the Zandars prodded me with a sharp elbow to the ribs and told me to get moving. As I scurried through the house, snatching up personal belongings, they continued to badger me with their insistent demands to "Hurry, hurry, hurry!" They forced me to turn over my house keys to them and barely gave me enough time to snatch up my two-year-old baby with one hand and a satchel with the other before pushing me out the door.

It all happened so quickly, that the shock came only in retrospect. All in an instant—as quickly as *that*—we had been robbed of our house, our freedoms, and all that we had always regarded as our birthright. In the same way that anyone in today's society would refuse to believe that such a thing were possible, we did not believe it then. Moving through the streets, I moved as if in a dream, for all of this *had* to be a dream! I believed that I would soon awaken in the comfort and warmth of my own bed, to see the sun shining through the window and the children amusing themselves with their playful pursuits.

But this was not to be. We had been organized with such speed and efficiency that even now we were being carried along on a wave of terror whose momentum and power would continue to build until at last it came crashing down upon us with a force that would sweep away six million, and subject many more to the horrors of a living death.

As we moved along, I found the combined weight of the baby and the suitcase extremely fatiguing. But whenever I would attempt to stop for a rest, the Zandars immediately closed in, kicking me with their heavy boots and ordering me to go on.

Finally, we reached the middle of town where the synagogue was located. As we entered this holy place, I was amazed to see it was overflowing with both local Jews and great numbers from other outlying areas. Since every seat had already been claimed, we settled for a spot on the cement floor and huddled together, attempting to avoid crowding others, which was virtually impossible. When the place had been filled far beyond its capacity, the doors were locked and soldiers were placed on guard throughout an interminable night of terror and suffering.

Since sleep was impossible, we milled about like frenzied cattle while the children wailed their hysterical protests and their parents sought vainly to comfort them.

There were many unpleasant sights to behold but none so pathetic as the elderly and bedridden who had been forced to come down to a place that had no means of accommodating their frail conditions. As the long night advanced, their pitiful cries pierced the mind with bizarre and frightful images, and it seemed to us that the ominous darkness would never pass. When at last it did, we were greeted by a militant announcement that we might visit a nearby outhouse in groups of twenty. As these groups began to form, we could only wonder if any mention would ever be made of food.

Immediately after our arrest, the children and I had sought out the company of Bertha, and insofar as this was possible, we attempted to stay together amid this great shifting mass of bodies.

"Can it be that it was all for nothing?" I heard Bertha mutter disconsolately and did not have to ask her what she meant. I already knew.

The soap business, the yard goods, the clandestine dressmaking activities of her daughters, had all these things merely sustained us so that we might now come to some wretched end? It hardly seemed possible, for that would serve to make living nothing more than an ironic joke. I preferred to think that we had been brought this far for a reason and that some higher power would continue to provide a way.

Even so, that way was not to be immediately forthcoming. Throughout the agony of our first full day in the temple, no human comforts or provisions were brought in. The more infirm among us could not survive such neglect, and several died. We had mixed feelings about that, thinking that perhaps these people had gotten the best of the bargain. Now they would no longer have to suffer.

And yet there were some small rewards. In a Catholic church a few miles away, a priest asked his congregation to deliver what food they could spare to the Jews in the temple, and around noon the next day these supplies began to arrive. I was both surprised and delighted to see a friend of my husband's, a local butcher, who brought us sausages, bacon and bread. By now, the children were totally ravenous and descended upon the food like a swarm of locusts. As a mother who had always taken pride in cooking hearty dishes for her children, it was difficult for me to observe such a heartbreaking scene.

Another friend who came to visit us while we were there was a Gypsy woman who in times past had occasionally done cleaning for me. She offered hard-boiled eggs and bread and, as I humbly accepted these things, I tried to forget that I had once berated Sol for extending credit to her people.

The Gypsies, of course, were also regarded as second-class citizens by the Nazis and would suffer many of the same indignities and physical torture the Jews did. At Dachau and Buchenwald, they would be selected for cruel experiments to determine, among other things, how long they could survive on salt water. Also, they would be forced to participate in large-scale sterilization programs, since the continued propagation of their race was not desired.

Suffice to say that, in the end, we would all forgo much in the way of human dignity merely to remain alive, although remaining alive these days had little to offer in the way of any real advantages.

A few days later, arrangements were made to transport us to Selvus, a community of approximately 12,000, where a Ghetto had been established solely for the incarceration of the Jews. Gentile families had been evacuated out of a four-square-mile area and a high fence was erected around this section to prevent escape. Eventually, 10,000 Jews would be forced to subsist here under heavy guard, and those who attempted to leave were shot on sight.

Our mode of transportation to the Ghetto in Selvus was both awkward and demeaning. Horse- and ox-drawn wagons were hastily assembled in front of the temple, and we were ordered to board in groups of ten to twelve per wagon. It was a long, tedious process, but at last it was done and we started on our way. With Zandars on horseback flanking us on both sides, we resembled nothing so much as a Gypsy caravan on its way to some unknown destination. We were not unaware of the curious stares we attracted from the residents of local Christian homes. They observed us discreetly from behind their curtained windows, but we were nonetheless conscious of their reactions. We sensed a certain amount of shock and amazement, and a great deal of genuine sorrow.

When we came through our own town, I began to get my bearings, realizing for the first time that we must be on our way to Selvus. As the wagons rumbled along, I became conscious of our predicament in yet another light. The community in which I had resided was known as a major railroad center, accommodating not only regional rail traffic but also that of such neighboring countries as Poland, Hungary and Romania. So it was altogether ironic that we, who had always considered ourselves to be sophisticated travelers, should now find ourselves bouncing along in an ox-drawn cart. I wished to believe that anything that followed this experience would have to be an improvement, although there was no guarantee of that. In that moment, the fear in my heart for the safety and continued survival of my children was truly indescribable.

When we arrived in Selvus, we were once again herded into a local temple. Since Jews from yet another town had already arrived there, the crowded conditions were even more stifling than before.

We spent another night without sanitary facilities or any other creature comforts, and the moaning and screaming that reverberated throughout that long, lonely night seemed to have increased a thousandfold.

It was a curious experience in one respect, for while we seemed to have nothing but time on our hands, there was little talk and even less speculation about what might lie ahead. It is difficult to explain our almost zombielike behavior, except to say that such luxuries as free speech and the right to protest were not available to us then as they are today. At the time of these events, no form of individual expression was condoned. You did not acquire such rights simply by demanding them. Rather, you could be instantly annihilated for even entertaining such a concept as equal rights since the Master Race had long since decided that no one was equal to them, and that the Jews were the most unequal of all.

Our second experience at being incarcerated in

a temple came to an end the following morning when the doors were opened and everyone was ordered out. We assembled, five in each line, with mothers carrying their small children, and proceeded to march through the town for a distance of approximately one mile. When we arrived at our destination we saw it was a vacant lot, and here we were commanded to stop and remained there for some time. We were finally divided into groups of eighty to 100 people per housing structure. With so many people in one building, we had to sleep on the floors and outside on the porches, but at least we were less confined than before. We were able to walk in the yard and could breathe fresh air, simple acts that by now had become rare privileges. Still, there was no food and no means of cleansing ourselves. Before long, we were all liberally infested with lice.

Meanwhile, I could not bear to hear the wretched pleas of my children.

"Mama, we want some bread and butter!"

"Mama, can we have some milk?"

My inability to provide them with their desires triggered my first real thoughts of suicide. It seemed to me that I had no further use in this world if I could not even supply these little ones with their basic needs.

After a couple days, some food was finally brought in, and we later learned it had been collected from the Jewish houses in the community. It was carefully rationed out and consisted mainly of potatoes, corn meal and wheat. We cooked everything in water and ate it just as it was. Later, whenever a load of grain arrived, it created instant bedlam.

We lived this way for six weeks and, in that short time, somehow became reconciled to living like animals and accepting human deprivation as a matter of course. To us, the attainment of a crust of bread was considered a victory, and our day-to-day survival itself was the greatest achievement of all.

At long last, we were once again ordered to form into lines and, in the company of heavily armed troops, were marched all the way to a train station several miles away. The thought of finally enjoying some decent transportation was enough to spur us on, but our spirits quickly fell when we saw the long line of cattle cars that awaited us. Once it had been filled, each car was taxed with eighty to ninety people, then padlocked securely from the outside. Air spaces were located at the tops of the cars, but these small windows were totally insufficient for the needs of so many people. Frantically seeking additional ventilation, we discovered small cracks here and there and huddled around these as best we could. Before the train departed, the doors were repositioned so that a small stream of air could enter through a thin crack, just enough to make the lungs scream for more.

With no room to stretch out or move about and no food or water, we traveled for two days and two nights in these cattle trains. Suffering itself required a certain amount of exertion, so we tried to remain as quiet as possible, but the agony of many was not to be denied. As they writhed and moaned on the floors of the cars, others relieved themselves in their shoes and then tried to dispose of their waste through the narrow windows up above.

The train stopped several times along its route. Each time it did, we screamed and begged our captors for water, but their only response was to shoot their rifles into the air and command us to be silent.

When this ghastly journey at last came to an end, the doors to the train were opened and we were abruptly ordered out. This was easier said than done, for after traveling so long in these cramped quarters, standing and walking were a near impossibility. Even so, the harsh German commands persisted.

"Unsteigen! Unsteigen!" Get off! Get off!

As we sought to obey, we stumbled and fell to the ground, and scrambled about on all fours while the officers struck us repeatedly with the butts of their rifles.

Soon afterward, a very curious process took place, a kind of sorting out of everyone on board. Elderly people, together with the very young, were ordered to congregate on one side while the older youths and middle-aged were ordered to another. When at last it was our turn, one of several Jewish prisoners assigned to assisting the German officers in unloading the passengers approached me and inquired about the relationship among our small group.

"This is Frau Weisberger, the grandmother of my children," I replied courteously, "and these are my daughters." I was cradling the two-year-old as the seven-year-old clung anxiously to the hem of my coat. Magda stood silently by, observing these proceedings with huge, somber eyes.

Suddenly, the Polish Jew reached out and, taking Lillian from me, placed her in my mother-in-law's arms. Then he disentangled Veronica's tiny fingers from my coat and urged her over to where Bertha stood. The child did not hesitate. She dearly loved her grandmother, and so readily entrusted herself to her care.

"What age is your oldest girl?" the prisoner asked me then. I told him that Magda was sixteen.

In a conspiratorial sort of way, he leaned forward and said, "Tell me that she is eighteen," and, as I considered this curious suggestion, he gestured for Magda and me to move off to the right.

While none of it made much sense at the time, we assumed it all had something to do with a reclassification process. Later, I would come to understand that the prisoner, in suggesting that I lie about Magda's age, had enabled me to spare her. No one under the age of eighteen was felt to be useful to the Reich, and Bertha was considered too old. The Jewish inmate who had been assigned to our detail knew that if I continued to remain standing there, holding little Lillian, that we would both be sent, along with the very young children and the elderly, to be gassed and then cremated. Since he had functioned in his present capacity for some time, he knew who was eligible for work and who would be selected for immediate disposal. It was an incredible quirk of fate that resulted in our survival that day, and on other occasions yet to come.

When at last our little group was dispersed, it marked our final parting, for while Magda and I would continue along on a journey which would finally lead us to Auschwitz, the quiet courage of Bertha and the purity and innocence of Veronica and baby Lillian would be lost to the diabolical expertise of the Nazi exterminators.

Once the elderly and very young children had been loaded into military trucks and driven away, we were again lined up five in a line and then ordered to march off in yet another direction.

"Marschieren! Marschieren!" the Germans shouted impatiently as we faltered in our tracks or glanced about curiously in an attempt to establish our whereabouts.

After we had covered a distance of approximately two miles, we suddenly approached seemingly endless rows of frame barracks, each individually fenced with electrified wire. Signs posted here and there identified this place as a Work

Camp, which was deceptively reassuring to many in our group. We took note of the sign that was the most prominently displayed:

ARBEIT MACHT FREI (Work Frees You).

It seemed to confirm our role as members of a work force, which was less objectionable than many of the things we had been imagining. While we were momentarily reassured, our hopes would soon be dashed. We had arrived at the entrance to the most infamous of all the extermination camps: Auschwitz! Early in 1940, it had been converted from a cavalry barracks into a so-called "quarantine camp." It contained four huge gas chambers and an adjoining crematorium which enabled it to surpass all others in the systematic death and disposal of human beings; toward the last, it was eliminating 6,000 victims a day. In a twisted attempt at good taste, its deadly secrets had been effectively disguised under well-manicured lawns with floral borders.

"Well, this is certainly better than the things I had heard," came a whispered comment from one member in our group. "Hard work might be a somewhat unpleasant experience, but at least it is not a fatal one."

Still, it struck me that there was an unnatural quality about the place, as there was no hint of the productive spirit that generally accompanies any efforts associated with either industry or war.

The community of Auschwitz itself was populated by approximately 12,000. It was a damp, marshy place where the ground never dried. It was also the site of a major synthetic coal-oil and rubber plant which had for a long time used cheap slave labor in the construction of new buildings and factory operations. It could easily have passed for a typical factory town except for the presence of so many stick-thin, shabbily dressed women with shaved heads who peered at us through the fences and begged for whatever scraps of food we might still have in our possession.

"Throw us whatever you have!" they begged. "They will take it all away from you anyway!"

Instinctively, Magda moved in closer beside me, and I sensed her terror at being verbally accosted by these strange creatures. Without hair, they all had a kind of mongoloid appearance and, while we preferred to think that they were only babbling nonsense, there was something oddly prophetic about them. We sensed that soon their fate and ours would become irrevocably intertwined, and that this experience would change us all for the balance of our days on this earth.

Men and women were separated at Auschwitz and, once this segregation process had been completed, we entered through a tall gate and were taken into a huge building where a number of German officers awaited us. As one might order another to open or close a window, these officers told us to undress and throw our clothes into a pile at our feet. It was not a request that encouraged immediate action. As we hesitantly stood about, trembling with fear and embarrassment, the stripping procedure was officially launched by an officer who rudely tore the dress from a woman close at hand. As she cried out in protest, the officers rewarded her with cold, sneering glances and the type of ribald laughter that is designed to reduce such unfortunate people to the level of a dirty joke.

Once we had all removed our clothing, we were closely inspected by the hard, critical eyes of these same officers, who poked and probed our bodies with an arrogant familiarity, as if defying us to voice some objection.

They examined us for signs of physical flaws or infections that might be serious enough to exempt us from service to the Reich. While being accepted was not the most pleasant prospect in the world, being rejected was even worse, for it meant certain death. While we did not know these things at the time, we continued to follow along and do as we were told, with a survivor's instinct that told us there was no other way.

We next assembled in an adjoining room, where a group of men and women quickly descended upon us with razors and shears. They shaved every part of our bodies with crude and clumsy haste, and when they were done, we were literally covered with nicks and cuts that burned and bled, only adding to our general misery. Throughout this degrading experience, Magda's eyes avoided my own, and I knew her humiliation was of a special kind. Heretofore, her young body had been pure and untouched. She had been raised to respect her own virtue and from this had suddenly fallen into the hands of a vile, callous stranger who shaved her pubic hair as casually as he might shave his own face.

Even had there been an opportunity to console her, there is little enough I could have said. The girl felt justifiably ashamed and violated. In that moment, it would have been ludicrous to remind her that at least she was still alive, because I knew she would have insisted she would be better off dead.

The order to go to the showers was a welcome one, although it did not provide the comfort we had sought. The showers had to be shared by ten women at a time, and the water was icy cold. Standing there, looking like plucked chickens, we shivered and avoided one another's eyes. In a matter of minutes, we had become exact replicas of the strange, ugly creatures that had greeted us at the fences. As a sudden wave of pessimism engulfed me, I began to feel we had finally reached our doom, that this place would be our cemetery, and that our time was not far off.

After we emerged from the showers, we were directed to yet another room where, in assembly line fashion, we were issued our meager wardrobe. As one woman handed us some panties, the next provided an undershirt, and finally, we were given a piece of ragged clothing that passed for a dress. The dresses had been stacked in a pile and were distributed according to their order rather than size. As a result, I received a long rayon dress that hung nearly to the floor, while Magda was given one that barely covered her.

The final indignity we were forced to endure was perhaps the most debasing of all. As we filed from the room, a man standing by the door with a bucket in one hand and a brush in the other, painted a long red stripe down our backs for purposes of easy identification.

By now, a cold drizzling rain had begun to fall, providing a soft melancholy sound that furnished a fitting accompaniment to our mood. Once again we were ordered to march through the slimy clay soil that threatened to suck us down with every step. Finally, we arrived at the barracks buildings in which we would be housed. Entering each building in groups of forty or fifty, we saw that other women were already there. They regarded us with little enthusiasm, and the reason for this was altogether obvious. Space was limited, and as our numbers increased, we would be forced to live together like sardines packed into a can.

Rows and rows of bunks stretched from the floor to the ceiling—they were little more than wide shelves, with as many as a dozen girls occupying each space. They slept on the bare boards and, since the width of the bunks was so narrow, they could only lie down to be even close to comfortable.

The bathroom facilities consisted of two large pails placed in one corner of the barracks. Since these were constantly overflowing, the buckets emitted a stench that was truly nauseating.

Amid this filth and squalor, we were destined to be reunited with certain loved ones, although the nature of our relationship would be drastically altered by these devastating events. My sister Blanche had been assigned to the same barracks Magda and I shared, but the rest of my family had long since been separated from us. Our hopes of ever seeing them again had already begun to wane.

On the morning of our second day in the barracks, Magda suddenly tugged at my sleeve and pointed toward another bunk with an air of restrained excitement.

"Look, Mama, it's Aunt Margaret!" As my eyes followed where she was pointing, I saw, huddled in a dark corner, a woman who vaguely resembled one of Bertha's daughters, although I could not be sure. She had the same buxom build but none of the statuesque grace. Without the aid of any supportive undergarments, her body flopped about grotesquely, and I sensed her mortification in being exposed in this way.

"Margaret, is it really you?" I asked, squinting hard into the darkness of her bunk.

Her body seemed to shrink away from me as I spoke, but at the same time, she tentatively extended her hand. Grasping it firmly, I tried to assure her with a simple touch that there was still someone familiar and caring for her to turn to. But her eyes did not warm with recognition, and I thought perhaps this might be due to my own wretched appearance.

"It's Shari," I explained quickly. "Shari and Magda."

She shook her head in doubt or disbelief, her nervous glance flickering over me in a strangely calculating way. She seemed to regard everything as a trap and jumped at the slightest sound.

Of course, we were under constant guard and this was one of the reasons for Margaret's anxiety, but just then, the German officers were all on the outside of the building, and I felt compelled to take advantage of the opportunity.

"Can you get us out of here?" Margaret asked suddenly, in a voice that was little more than a whimper.

"Eventually we will all be released," I hastened to assure her. "This is only a work camp. It has been formed to aid the war effort. The war cannot last forever."

A moon-faced Jewish Pole in the bunk above snorted disdainfully at that and, climbing down from her perch, proceeded to use one of the makeshift toilets with a flagrant openness that clearly expressed her contempt for my ignorance.

"Wherever did you hear such a fairy tale as that?" She sneered. "Don't you know where you are? Don't you know what this place is?"

It occurred to me then that the others shared some knowledge I did not. They were all grinning in a mirthless, sinister way, and I felt a chill run through me that had nothing to do with the temperature outside.

"This is Auschwitz!" she snapped with angry impatience. "They do strange and wonderful things here. They can make people disappear—just like magic! Everyday, you will have an opportunity to be one of those people. Soon, you will begin to wonder if one fate is truly better than another, for at least those who are already gone no longer have an ax hanging over their heads."

Instinctively, I clapped my hands over Magda's ears, but the way the child's eyes seemed to widen endlessly revealed that the impact of the Polish woman's words had already done their damage.

"Your friend Margaret knows all about it," the woman jeered with a quick nod toward the cowering figure in the bunk. "She knows what all that black smoke out there means. Why don't you ask her?"

"I've heard that there are factories around here," I responded reasonably. "Auschwitz is an industrial city, is it not?"

"It is industr*ious*, not industrial," the woman retorted with a sharp laugh. "It is determined to meet its quota of gassing more Jews to death than any other extermination camp in operation. Those loved ones no longer with you have already gone to help fill that quota."

"*No!*" I cried, in one last desperate attempt to keep any of this from being real.

The Polish woman sidled over to me then, a sly, treacherous smile parting her thick lips in a way that gave her a truly unpleasant countenance. "When you were first taken from the trains, what do you think all of that 'you to the left,' 'you to the right' business was about? Whatever members of your family were separated from you then were either too young or too old to participate in the so-called 'war effort.' You and your girl are the right age, and strong enough to do their dirty work—at least for a while. When you no longer can, you will meet the same fate as the others."

A powerful range of emotions surged through me then: rage, violence, fear and something that bordered on all-out hysteria. But I saw at once I could not give in to any of them, because Magda's face had gone totally white. As she swayed and fell to the floor, I ran to her side and quickly tried to revive her. Several women attempted to assist, and in the background, I could hear another in our group severely chastising the Polish woman who had caused all of this. "Why do you take out your bitterness on this innocent child? She has nothing to do with any of it. You're a miserable old bitch who has a talent for nothing more than making a bad thing even worse."

Under different circumstances, this tense atmosphere might easily have progressed into a physical free-for-all, but as it was, the Polish woman had to content herself with throwing hateful glances at the rest of us, after which she retired once again to her bunk.

Once Magda had regained consciousness, she soon remembered all the things that had been said, and anxiously looked to me for confirmation or denial.

"Is it *true*?" she asked, in a small, pathetic voice. "Have they murdered Veronica and Lillian—and Grand-mama?"

"We can't be sure of that," I said, pulling her to me and rocking her gently back and forth. "In a place like this, you hear many things. We cannot afford to believe everything we hear."

It was a futile, even absurd attempt at reassurance, for Magda had only to look into my eyes to know that I believed it too.

At the outset, life at Auschwitz was a curious experience. We were not immediately assigned to a work detail, as we had expected. Instead, we were confined to our barracks, existing on a meager ration of black coffee and a slice of bread for breakfast, no lunch and a pot of some dreadful excuse for vegetable soup in the evening. The soup was weak and watery, containing only a few wilted vegetable leaves, some potatoes and a considerable amount of sand. Each bunk had to share a small pot of this nauseating fare and, since we hadn't any spoons, we each took a swallow or two and continued to pass the bowl around until the soup was gone. At first, there were those who flatly refused to eat it, insisting it was simply too vile for human consumption. Margaret was one of these. Each time the soup was offered, she would merely stare at it, and then collapse into a fit of nervous giggling. I did not care for the sound of it. It had an uncontrollable quality to it and, over a period of time, began to sound slightly deranged. Still, I would not permit myself to believe that Margaret was actually losing her mind. She was a lovely, sensitive soul whose mental and emotional balance had been taxed to the limit. Given enough time, I was sure she would be more like her old self again.

Even so, she continued to eye us critically as we dipped our hands into the soup pot and groped about for whatever sediments of food we could find. I felt somewhat intimidated by her, because it could not be denied that we had become almost animal-like in our efforts to survive. Our newly adopted eating habits could perhaps be most accurately compared to those of a cow we had once had on the family farm who, as a treat, occasionally received a large pail of bran and potatoes moistened with warm water. She would attack this delicacy in much the same way we now assaulted our meals in the camp. The cow at least had been permitted the luxury of dining alone.

Magda spent what time she could with her beloved aunt, attending to her in small ways and trying to brighten her spirits.

"Come, Aunt Margaret, have a swallow of soup. You must keep up your strength or you will become ill."

But Margaret would have none of it. "Do they really expect us to eat that?" she would say with a sarcastic smirk, and then dissolve into gales of fitful laughter. By now her behavior could be termed eccentric and, while I did not care to see it in this light, I no longer had a choice.

As inmates continued to arrive, we were joined by a childhood friend of Magda's. Her name was Eva Jozsef, or Shajndu, as she was referred to in Yiddish. The two girls had enjoyed many happy times together, playing hopscotch and ball in the shade of the tallest trees. There were many apple, pear and plum trees in Shajndu's yard that regularly bore succulent fruit the girls would pick for use in favorite family recipes. They would also play hide-and-seek in the hayloft, and trade stories and girlhood confidences as close friends are inclined to do. Magda and Shajndu attended elementary school together and had completed the fifth grade by the time the war broke out. The Czech schools were soon replaced with Ruthenian schools, which required the girls to learn to speak Ruthenian and to master the Russian alphabet. They adjusted to this without difficulty, but soon the Hungarians took over and, in order for Magda to enter junior high school, she was required to pass a rather difficult examination. With the aid of a tutor, she studied for this test for an entire semester and managed to pass it successfully, whereupon she completed junior high without further problems.

Her friend Shajndu's family included two brothers and one sister. She was the only member of this family to make it to Auschwitz. The rest, with the exception of her younger brother, were immediately taken to the crematorium. After the war, her brother would return home, a victim of tuberculosis, and for the rest of his life, remain in delicate health.

Magda's reunion with Shajndu in the concentration camp was a bittersweet occasion. They were a great comfort to one another but became extremely despondent whenever their reminiscences would force them to compare what had been to what was. The past now seemed like a beautiful dream, only a figment of the imagination. The grim reality of life was what we were surrounded with each day, and this was what we had to cope with.

Each morning we endured a five a.m. roll call, at which time we were required to line up and be counted, a long, tedious process that was repeated again in the evening. With thirty barracks housing 32,000 women, it was not unusual for the entire procedure to take several hours, particularly if everyone could not be accounted for. At the same time, each prisoner was carefully reviewed for any signs of weakness or ill health. Since Margaret's behavior was becoming increasingly bizarre, I would hope and pray each time that she would manage to conduct herself with some semblance of normalcy, since any sort of odd behavior would most assuredly cost her her life. Magda and I repeatedly cautioned her to act discreetly, but it never discouraged her shrill, reckless laughter, and so at last I was forced to accept that she had become mentally unbalanced.

Of all the discomforts we had to endure, the daily roll call was one of the most physically taxing. Regardless of the weather, we would be required to stand for hours, waiting for everyone to be accounted for. If someone chose to hide or attempted an escape, we were all punished for it just as if we had been a party to this person's transgressions. We would be denied our morning coffee and generally endured additional privations which continued to sap the strength and general health of many who were later removed from the lines and taken away to the gas chambers.

The roll call was supervised by two of the most ruthless and feared of the Nazi staff members: Irma Grese and Dr. Josef Mengele.

Irma Grese was an attractive young girl with an angelic, heart-shaped face and a satanic mission in life. She, like many of the women assigned to the supervision of the concentration camps, proved to be far more heartless in her dealings with the prisoners than her male counterparts. In the winter of 1945, she would be sentenced to death for her participation in Nazi war crimes, although other girls who were tried along with her received much lighter sentences.

But Dr. Josef Mengele was the ultimate example of heartless brutality, and in the Auschwitz-Birkenau murder camps, came to be known as the infamous "angel of death." It was not uncommon for him to meet the new arrivals at the Birkenau railroad ramp near Auschwitz, where he would personally select victims for the gas chambers.

He had a formidable appearance, what with his head of jet-black hair, a neatly trimmed moustache and a steely gaze that immediately aroused fear in the hearts of everyone who was forced to meet it. His calculating scrutiny of people made them feel that he must be considering them for the cruel butchery he preferred to think of as medical experimentation. He was best known for his research into the genetics of twins, a project he pursued with frightful results at Birkenau.

Still, Mengele's primary job was to select people for the death chambers and, even while engaged in supposedly compassionate acts, he somehow managed to reap destruction. On one occasion, when inmates at a camp for which he had medical responsibility complained of lice, Mengele ordered the barracks fumigated, and destroyed both the lice and the people.

The very sight of him plunged an icy dagger through my heart, particularly since I believed

Margaret's strange behavior could not long escape his attention. Although she did not always seem to be in touch with reality, she maintained a certain clarity about the events that occurred at the time Bertha and my younger children were taken away.

"I must go and help them," she would insist at times. "I must go where they are. Mother is too old to tend to such small children alone."

Although Magda and I would attempt to divert her attention to other things, she was determined to return to this subject at every available opportunity.

Her reluctance to eat was a growing source of concern to us, and the problem was eventually compounded by our sudden introduction to Limburger cheese. It was a totally foreign substance to us, and its rank odor made us inclined to associate it with the odor of human waste we were forced to live with every day.

Margaret, with the proud superiority of a professional chef who had once catered elegant parties, again insisted that this was something unfit for human consumption. We tried to make her understand we were no longer in a position to pick and choose what we would eat, that now we ate simply in order to survive, emphasizing that she must learn to do the same.

Still, Margaret had plans of her own and, had we known what they were, perhaps we might have been able to dissuade her. Still, we did *not* know, and so stood by in helpless and horrified silence as Margaret asserted herself one morning during roll call. As the weak and sickly were being taken from the lines, Margaret suddenly stepped forward, too, insisting that she be included. In her confused and highly disturbed condition, she believed she would be taken to a camp where the elderly and younger children were being kept. In volunteering herself, she hoped to be reunited with Bertha and the children, but of course was immediately taken to the gas chambers.

In the days that followed, I could not erase the picture of how she had run along behind the others, exhibiting an innocent, almost childlike trust as she waved her arms and cried out, "Wait for me! Wait for me! "

And as if to emphasize this horrible image in my mind, we were constantly enmeshed in a veil of thick, suffocating smoke that produced a stench with its own uniquely caustic qualities. This flesh-burning incense assailed our eyes and nostrils with an unrelenting fervor, although breathing it made the truth of the situation no more real to us. It was simply inconceivable to think—to *know*—that these ovens were being fed with our friends, our relatives, our children, families from which we had sprung, and those we had married into. What a hideous fire! For only a devil's cauldron could require a constant diet of human life; annihilating forever the most loving hearts, the most courageous ones; eradicating creative artists, intellectual giants and every other form of talent and human potential with mindless abandon.

We tried not to think about it, but there was nothing else to think about. The stench seared through our lungs and into our hearts and minds, with a ghastly message that could no longer be ignored or denied. *We would not be the same after this!* Already, we were learning to accept the unacceptable. We were changing in a way that made it possible to endure and survive amid such devastation . . . to drink our coffee . . . to eat our soup . . . to stand in line . . . to sleep and talk and, occasionally, to even contemplate some kind of future.

In the Ghetto, I had watched the children changing, amusing themselves with new and terrible games, conducting mock funerals, playing at grave-digging, and appointing themselves official gatekeepers of the Ghetto. These games now came as naturally to them as tag and hide-and-seek, and they seemed to derive as much enjoyment from them.

My own surviving daughter was changing, too. Her somber, haunted eyes had seen horrifying images that could never be erased. If she survived, these memories would survive with her. I feared they would taint and twist her future in a way that would make it impossible for her to ever again be truly happy, well-adjusted, trusting or optimistic. I had heard about the resiliency and adaptability of children, but surviving a broken home or occasional physical abuse could not be compared to this. Nothing could be compared to this! Perhaps, in the end, Magda's mind would snap as Margaret's had. She looked so frail and vulnerable to me, like a straw in the wind in her thin, ragged dress. I realized suddenly that in all truth, I wished only to survive for her—for as long as she did—until the end came. It seemed to me that if we managed to remain together, we could endure, somehow finding the strength to face whatever God had in store for us, and accepting it as His will.

4

In the coming days and weeks, our lives at Auschwitz proceeded with monotonous regularity. It was a generally depressing and uneasy experience, for there was no way to know in what frightening manner it might suddenly be altered. Constantly living on the brink of such a large question had the effect of amplifying the importance of small, everyday occurrences. Not knowing if each crust of bread might be our last gave this hard, stale substance a special flavor. And the smoke-laden air was a constant reminder that life was precious, not only in terms of a normal span of years, but every hour and every moment of it. Even the gloomiest, rainiest day—and there were many of them—held out a shred of promise for those who survived each one without being taken to the gas chambers. Meanwhile, the purposeless routine went on in keeping with the schedule that had been established for the camp.

Auschwitz had been separated into individual blocks of barracks. Each block had an alphabetical designation and the barracks themselves were numbered. Magda, Blanche and I had been confined in Block C, Barracks Number 10. The barracks on either side of us were separated from ours by high fences which had been liberally laced with electrified wire. Each barracks building existed as a separate community. We were not allowed to converse with any inmates from the other barracks, and our conduct was closely monitored to ensure that this rule would not be violated.

As many as a thousand girls were housed in each unit, with only the clothes on their backs and virtually nothing in the way of hygienic facilities. It was not to be believed that such a way of life could continue for more than an hour or a day, and yet it continued on and on. We pressed in upon one another like frenzied cattle, conscious of one another's breathing and the constant, suffocating closeness. We moved about aimlessly, without direction or purpose, until the milling became too complicated or tiresome. There was little conversation. Talk seemed futile, as futile as everything else in this state of monstrous confinement.

Still, some bleak hope continued to exist in the midst of so much devastation—in my own heart, and in the heart of my one surviving child. But my sister Blanche was another matter. Her outlook was less optimistic. On one particular day, she became reflective about her life and the various opportunities she had missed.

"At any rate, it is fortunate I never married," she said with a heavy sigh. "You were always unhappy about that, Shari. But now you can see it was for the best."

I hardly knew how to answer her. In theory, she was right. Yet, I had always wished for her what one would wish for anyone, that she might have the love and comfort of a devoted husband and the added joy of beautiful, healthy children. In such an environment, the softer side of her nature would have had a chance to evolve. As it was, she had developed something of a hard outer shell, a kind of militant attitude that disguised the warm, compassionate soul underneath.

Blanche was tall, large-boned and stocky. Her hair was dark and her skin had a much deeper tone than mine. We would not have been taken for sisters by anyone who sought a family resemblance, but we were close in the ways that mattered most, each offering to the other what sustenance we could, if only through one another's presence.

"When this is all over," I told her, "you will have another chance at life and living. You are still young. You mustn't speak as if everything were over."

"It is over," she said, with a certainty that was

truly alarming, for the manner in which she spoke had no edge of madness to it. It was not the way it had been with Margaret. Blanche was merely expressing an opinion, based on her own ability to come to a reasonable conclusion. In the past, she had frequently settled friendly family arguments in much the same way, injecting her infuriating logic at precisely the proper moment. And to the extent that I had admired her objectivity then, I truly feared it now.

"Blanche, you mustn't speak this way. There is always hope. Hope is what we cling to when all else is gone. We have been through so much and survived it all. There is always a chance."

Blanche looked about to see where Magda was. When she saw that the girl was not within earshot, she said, "I know you feel an obligation to the child to remain optimistic. And, of course, there is even a possibility you may be right. But I wasn't speaking of you, dear sister. I was speaking of me. It is something I sense, I feel, I *know* to be true. Don't ask me how or why. Perhaps, at the last, one is given a glimmer of foresight as a means of preparing for things to come."

"I won't listen to any more of this!" I protested angrily. "It is pointless to talk that way. Haven't we enough to contend with without your pessimistic predictions? If it happens, it happens! But there isn't any need to dwell on it. I would have expected more of you than that. This is idiotic, crazy talk!"

As I turned my back on her and abruptly moved away, I could not help but notice that, despite my outburst, her composure remained intact. I had called her idiotic and crazy, and yet any impartial observer would have been forced to conclude that in this instance, Blanche was behaving more rationally than I. I did not wish to analyze what this might mean, since her side of the argument was simply too horrible to consider.

There was no denying that our continued incarceration was taking its toll. We all felt we should have been assigned to some work detail long before now, and that our enforced idleness was not a good sign.

In the humid heat of spring, quarrels erupted over trivial matters. While one girl was accused of taking up too much space in her bunk, another was chastised for swallowing more than her share of the soup. Each morning and evening, we were organized for the count, trying desperately to look hale and hearty enough to pass inspection for another day. This effort was beyond the capabilities of many and was rapidly taking its toll on Magda. In recent weeks, she had grown so weak, so frail and unsteady on her feet that I feared she could not continue to tolerate the interminable hours of standing. Each time we were finally permitted to return to the barracks, she would sink wearily into her bunk, pale and trembling with hunger and fatigue. It was something of a double-edged sword to wish that we might be put to work, however, because while this might extend the lives of some, it would most assuredly shorten the lives of many others. In her present state, I could not think of a single chore Magda would be capable of performing. Her large, dark eyes were now the most dominant feature in her face, overshadowing the pale, sunken cheeks and the thin frail line of her mouth. Her limbs were mere pipestems, appearing too fragile to support her, and her skin was a sickly ashen color. During the night, if she slept too soundly, too quietly, I would move in against her and listen for her breathing. Each time she would stir or open her eyes, I would think to myself, Thank God—she still lives!

And then, one morning, news made the rounds that we would soon be assigned to various work details, a cruel irony of life—or so it seemed to me. Now, after weeks of being denied the nourishment and care required to build a productive work force, we would be assigned to some grueling task to test the last of our reserves. What did the Nazis hope to accomplish with such a motley crew of weak and starving scraps of humanity who barely had the strength to survive another roll call?

On the appointed day, I was quickly dispatched to a transport that contained a group numbering a thousand or more, while another smaller group of about five hundred was assembled from the tallest individuals amongst us. Owing to her stature and build, Blanche was quickly assigned to the latter group, and this left Magda's fate yet to be decided.

As I prayed for her to be sent over to us, I saw a sight that momentarily stopped my heart, causing an inner reaction that was like a strange, silent screaming. I watched her *being herded in with the weaker ones,* the ones considered no longer fit to survive! It was the final nightmare, like watching her walk into the jaws of a lion. It couldn't be happening, and yet it was! She was being taken from me, as Veronica and Lillian had been. Another swift, indifferent decision had been made; the officer responsible had already turned his back on her and moved away. As I watched, he exchanged some words with another uniformed German, and I could not believe it when he tossed back his head and laughed. Killing and laughter . . . laughter and killing. It was not to be believed. It was beyond any horror I could ever have imagined. Furthermore, it could not be condoned! I refused to accept this, the loss of this last beautiful child to the whims of these militant murderers.

Wishing to do a hundred things at once, I forced myself to remain perfectly still, to analyze the situation with a kind of desperate cunning. There were officers everywhere, but also a great deal of confusion. Perhaps I could use it to my advantage. The thought had barely formed itself in my mind when I recklessly stepped forward and, grabbing Magda by the arm, quickly pulled her into my group. To give her a place in line, I shoved another girl out of my row. Later, when the officers made a final inspection and saw that one of the lines was longer than the rest, they removed a girl from the rear and sent her off with another party.

It was not until we were instructed to march that I dared to admit to myself that Magda had been spared. For a few more hours, perhaps another day, she had been spared. It would give me some time to think, to devise another ploy, if another ploy were needed. And it seemed altogether likely. Magda's face had gone chalky white, she seemed close to fainting, and I knew she would not be able to walk any great distance.

I was able to breathe a little easier when I saw the train station up ahead. Once there, we boarded another cattle train—forty to a car—with two SS officers guarding each compartment. Since no mention was made of our ultimate destination, it remained the mystery it had always been, and once again had the effect of turning our bones to jelly and our blood to ice water.

The train slowly proceeded on its journey amid grim speculation clearly mirrored in the eyes of its terrified passengers. The presence of the officers did not permit conversation, but messages still passed between us in somber looks, soft whimpers, sad sighs of resignation and low, muffled moans.

The following morning, the train stopped in the midst of a thick forest where we were ordered off and told to line up and wait for the next command. In so remote an area as this it was impossible to sustain any further hope of survival. We were all united in the thought that we had been brought here as part of some diabolical plan that could only end in mass murder. When we were once again ordered to march, we did so with the certainty that we were at last marching to our deaths. On every side of us, the path was lined with Gestapo soldiers pointing their raised rifles. Anticipating a shot with every step, we moved forward with a kind of fatalistic cadence, looking straight ahead.

My peripheral vision permitted brief glimpses of Magda, and I found myself thinking that these would be the last that I would ever have of her. But just then, my fantasies won out over reality. In my mind's eye, she was not wearing a thin ragged dress that the hot, dry wind whipped sharply against her spindly legs and her pale, drawn face no longer harbored those huge, dark-circled eyes. She was glowing and beautiful, with long, shining curls, moving elegantly in a soft, chiffon party dress, the picture of confidence and good health.

The road ahead became blurred with tears as I considered the many pleasurable experiences in life she would never know. The rightful legacy of youth had been denied her, and soon, life itself would be denied her—as quickly as the armed officers decided to empty their rifles into us.

The waiting became unbearable, triggering a

desire to cry out, *"Shoot us!* Shoot us now and have done with it!"

But even as these wild impulses raged through me, I noticed a sign that read *STUTHOFFER VALD* (Stuthoffer Forest) and soon afterward, another camp came into view, similar to Auschwitz, but smaller.

High-ranking officers awaited us at the gate and, as we entered the yard, we were once again counted and then ordered to sit down on the sandy ground. Later, we would learn we were close to the Baltic Sea, near Danzig, an odd region topographically, with an almost desertlike terrain. It was mid-July, and the sun beat down unmercifully on our shaved heads, and being forced to sit on the red hot sand was an excruciating experience. We endured nearly two hours of it, although a number of women with weak hearts had fainted by the time the next order came. They received no assistance from the officers, who finally commanded us to line up two in a row and march ahead to a spot where a soldier stood beside a large iron kettle. As we passed by in a double row, he gave each pair of girls a bowl of soup to share. Once we had again settled ourselves on the ground, we hastily devoured this unexpected meal, surprised to find it a great improvement over what we had grown accustomed to. The thicker stock seemed to have a barley base, and we were even given spoons to eat it with.

Afterward, we were again ordered to line up and

then were marched between long lines of barracks, where the first two rows of girls were ordered inside to the showers.

Although our entrance into the camp involved procedures similar to those at Auschwitz, there were certain improvements, not the least of which was the clothing we were given. Our spirits were buoyed by the feel of clean underwear against our skin and the gray and blue striped prison uniforms that replaced our ill-fitting dresses. It felt so good to be clean again, it was like a small miracle! Once we had been assigned to our barracks, we regarded one another with open amazement, for we had never expected to make it this far.

The next morning, we were awakened by a five o'clock bugle call and once more were subjected to the tedious roll call procedures we had endured at Auschwitz. It seemed to me that the entire matter could have been more efficiently organized. From time to time, the officers would lose count and have to start over, which automatically added several more hours to the entire process. But not until it was completed were we allowed to sit down on the ground and drink a cup of black coffee. The suffocating heat throughout the day proved fatal to many of the women who quickly succumbed to heatstroke.

To have your life spared at the cost of every other form of human dignity and pride is less of a victory than one might imagine.

Being constantly threatened or beaten into submission had the effect of first cowing the spirit and, eventually, the very essence of the individual. The quality of self-esteem no longer existed among us, and I could only wonder about what psychological damage had been done to any who might survive.

Because of her recent narrow brush with death, I could see Magda had now retreated even further into herself. We did not speak of the terrifying moments during which she was selected for the group considered unworthy of survival or of the freakish combination of circumstances that had permitted me to snatch her back in time. Only the confusion of the moment and the infinite mercy of God had prevented us from both being sentenced to death on the spot. It was an experience that could not be acknowledged in words, because that would make it too terrifyingly real to endure. But we were aware of little else in the days that followed, and I knew that Magda often dreamed of it. She would frequently awaken with a start, with a wild, hysterical look in her eyes.

The methodical cruelty of the SS officers was all the more frightening because of their air of indifference. This heinous army of terror's impulsive acts could strike at any moment for any reason—or even for no reason at all. In the way they now totally controlled our lives, it was difficult to accept their humble beginnings.

Initially, their role in history had been small, barely perceptible. In January 1933, the Secret State Police functioned as nothing more than bodyguards to Hitler. It had drawn its recruits from the remains of the illegal Freikorps, a band of guerilla fighters who were part of defeated Imperial Germany.

The SS had been Hitler's own creation and, as such, he imposed upon it an internal discipline and an exaggerated sense of loyalty that made it the ideal instrument in his quest for total power.

The history of the SS was, of course, irrevocably interwoven with the life and career of Heinrich Himmler, who made it the dreaded war machine it was fated to become.

On the surface, he seemed extremely ill-suited for the role, what with his mild-mannered, bespectacled appearance. He had been a chicken farmer and continued to impress one as a chicken farmer, what with his high, thin hairline and weak, receding chin. Of course, it might have been these very physical shortcomings that spurred a deep inner desire to achieve outstanding feats of heroism and power. He greedily absorbed every facet of Nazism, from its imperialistic dreams to its so-called high purpose of annihilating one entire race to celebrate the birth of another Super Race that was to be the product of historical necessity.

From the beginning, Himmler saw the SS as a perfect instrument with a divine purpose. Performing its duties with honor, it was also obliged to perform them with a certain quality of elegance. This was reflected in the cut and style of the uniforms and in the noble mannerisms and hierarchial discipline of its members. The SS was intended to draw men from noble, even princely blood who could perform brutal tasks with dignified efficiency, thus lending an aura of high ideals to their truly appalling acts.

In the course of its activities, these ideals were fated to become fiendishly perverted. In 1931, this militantly inspired cause was to be further influenced by a most formidable supporter, the intellectual technocrat, Reinhard Heyrich. Possessed of an icy, amoral character, he was propelled by deep personal resentments kindled by his dishonorable discharge from the navy. He found the SS the perfect vehicle for his frustrated ambitions. Although he was not well-liked within the SS, he did more than anyone else under Himmler to assure the success of this army of terror.

Hitler's ascent into power would not have been possible without the SS. It was the very essence of the illegal fuehrer state which, through the efforts of Himmler, successfully took control of the police and began building up the concentration camps. Initially, the camps had been justified as places to provide protective custody for political suspects. Some of these camps were declared official under the Minister of the Interior, but others were unauthorized and totally controlled by the SS.

Once Hitler had gained the title Chancellor of the Reich, he no longer had any reason or inclination to operate within the law. Having successfully tested his ability to break constitutional laws, he began to vent his murderous ambitions and rebelled against his own people, insisting he was no longer accountable to any tribunal. Unfortunately, he was given a free rein to operate, and so came to understand that the legal state could be safely overpowered through intimidation. This, in itself, was fuel for the continued advancement of the SS, which was quickly declared immune from investigation by the law courts, and the concentration camps became places of execution without benefit of trial or appeal.

The horrible atrocities of Hitler's war were all the work of the SS, and their barbarism had become a systematically ruthless machine by the time we were exposed to it.

An altogether pointless side effect of our constant travail existed in my own tendency to reflect upon certain unalterable facts, not the least of which involved my mother's hesitancy to follow my father to the United States. There were times when I wanted to blame her for everything that had happened to us, although she could not possibly have foreseen the current horrendous course of events. Still, it continued to rankle that we had forgone our one opportunity to escape this devastation, because it was now clear we would have to pay an extremely high price for our folly.

My sister Sarah, who had accompanied my father on his last trip to America, had married and remained there, although my father eventually returned. And, of course, Pearl had been fortunate enough to meet Louis Stein who had provided *her* passport to freedom. It was a comfort to know that at least these two sisters were safe. On the other hand, I knew too that my older brother, David, who had remained behind with his wife and two children, would have met the same fate as Magda and I. Of that I had no doubt, although there was no way to confirm my suspicions. Our chances for survival were poor to nonexistent in this nightmare of suffering and horror, from which there was no escape except one.

Late at night as I lay half-asleep, half-awake, I would sometimes regress into my own childhood, recalling the gentle warmth of the aromatic spring air and the serene beauty of the picturesque landscape I had once called home.

I remembered the last time my father had returned to us, when I was about ten years old. The train on which he traveled did not stop in our village but rather in a neighboring community where my paternal grandfather lived. Knowing that my father would visit there for a while, I took it upon myself to go on foot to this neighboring village so that I might be the first to greet him.

Since I had only one pair of serviceable shoes, I was compelled to make the journey barefooted and, when at last I arrived at my grandfather's house, this was the first thing my father noticed.

As he picked me up and swung me happily into the air, he said in a mildly chastising tone, "Shari, my dear, is this any way to present yourself at your grandfather's house? Haven't you any shoes?"

I humbly explained that I had only one pair and they had to be saved for special occasions and school. I had not meant for this remark to reflect unfavorably upon him, but saw at once the impact it had. The saddest expression I have ever seen crossed his face, although he was not to blame for the privations we endured. Wartime regulations had not permitted him to correspond with us or send us money.

But now, with Magda lying here beside me, I could readily identify with my father's despair in not being able to provide for his children. It seemed to be a curse we were fated to pass on from one generation to the next.

My one concern at the moment was to get enough food into Magda to give her some strength and improve her appearance. Each daily roll call was cause for great anxiety, since it forced us to relive the moment she had been selected for extermination. And because this had happened once, it was not inconceivable it could happen again. I shared with her every morsel of food that came my way, insisting that my own appetite was poor, and that adults did not need nearly the amount of nourishment children did.

"But you aren't eating *anything*, Mama," Magda would point out now and again. "Here, I will eat a bite if you do."

After approximately two weeks, we went through a registration process which raised some questions that had not come up before. We were asked by our interrogators to identify ourselves and give the names of our hometowns, which made the entire procedure somewhat more humane. No one had yet expressed any interest in where we were from, and we gave our answers with a kind of nostalgic pride.

But the feeling of having become more real to our captors was short-lived, for on our way out the door we were each given numbered armbands to wear. My number was 39,439 and Magda's was 39,440. The bands were white linen with blue numbers on them, and the figures themselves were indicative of how many women were incarcerated there.

After we had all been assigned our armbands, we were once again instructed to line up for another inspection. We were to be selected for various jobs according to our capabilities and, as the selection process began, a cold chill once again ran through my body. Even before I saw it being done, I sensed what was going to happen. As one of the officers paused in front of Magda and evaluated her with sharp, critical eyes, I knew that she was going to be rejected once more. Even as this thought formed, I saw him pull her from the line.

Auschwitz! That dreaded word was back in our lives! She was on her way back to that hellhole of horror, and I knew that this would be her final journey.

I remembered the ploy that had worked before. It was insane to believe it might work again, but there was nothing else to do. *I can't let you go, my precious child!* I vowed in silent anguish, *I must keep you with me, or all is lost! If I lose you, my Magda, I don't care if I live another minute.*

Praying for the wisdom to act at the right moment, I quickly moved forward and yanked her into my group as the selection process continued. Clutching her bony arm with desperate determination, I closed my eyes and held my breath, certain I had not escaped detection this time. When I next dared to look about, I saw the officers had moved farther away, and that they were still totally preoccupied with their deadly game of selecting and rejecting. Once their work was done, they again noticed an extra girl in our line, and so pulled out another unfortunate victim from the rear.

We were then locked into our barracks for the balance of the day, giving us time to speculate about our future work assignments.

As the other women discussed ways their services might be used, Magda moved away from the group and stared blindly out the window. The day was gray and cloudy, aptly reflecting the mood of the moment. I crossed to her side, easily envisioning the dark thoughts that plagued her now. At every turn, she seemed marked for annihilation. These last-minute reprieves could not be expected to continue indefinitely.

"Don't think about it," I murmured softly as I came up behind her. "You have been spared. That is all that matters."

She turned toward me then and her expression was bleak. "That *isn't* all that matters!" she said. "What about the others? The ones who were sent in my place?"

"You are assuming the worst, my child. You can't be sure where they were sent."

"I am sure. And so are you, Mama. Other people are being killed so I might live. I'm not sure I care for life on those terms. Perhaps it would be best if they would take me."

"Stop it!" I cried in shock and horror at her very suggestion. "Don't ever let me hear you talk like that again!"

"Why not?" she asked listlessly. "What right have I to remain on this earth at the expense of others?"

"And what of your sisters? What of Aunt Margaret? What of the many losses our own family has suffered? We have earned the price of your survival many times over. Even Blanche is gone. I would like to believe she was taken to another camp, but I haven't any real hopes we will ever be reunited. There is nothing for us to believe in now except one another. You are here, and I am here. That is the only certainty left in the world for us."

"Yes, well, it may not always be so. You must prepare yourself for that, Mama."

"Never! We will survive together or perish the same way. Now, let's not speak of it again."

There was, in fact, little opportunity to resurrect that particular topic of discussion even if we had wanted to, for our part in the war effort had now officially begun.

The following day, at noon, we were taken from the barracks and ordered to march a distance of approximately two miles, where at last we came to a large building. As we filed through the door, two in a row, we were once again ordered to remove all of our clothing. After this had been done, we were subjected to yet another humiliating physical examination. The standards for survival were becoming more stringent now. Even those with mild rashes or blemishes were quickly removed from the lines.

Those of us who managed to pass inspection were next ordered to enter another room for a steam bath. We remained in this hot, humid enclosure the entire night, and it was an ordeal that many did not survive.

The following morning, we received a shirt, panties, a dress and then our shoes were returned to us. After that, we were once again lined up outdoors, and stepping out of the steam heat into that cold morning air caused many to suffer the effects of influenza and pneumonia.

We were next marched down to a depot where a freight train awaited us, along with soldiers who were standing by with three large crates of food. As we boarded the train, we were each given a piece of bread, a pat of margarine and a slice of sausage. Since we had not seen any food for twenty-four hours, it was difficult to resist wolfing down this meager ration. But we had already been warned that we had a long trip ahead of us, so we nibbled at our snack with appropriate discretion.

The journey took two nights and one day, and we arrived at our destination on a Sunday morning. It was becoming increasingly difficult to keep track of time but, as near as I could tell, these events were taking place during the latter part of July 1944.

We hadn't any means of determining where we were, but wherever it was, we soon came upon another empty camp and later learned that we were somewhere in Poland. Gestapo officers were waiting for us. They herded us into barracks consisting of smaller rooms than we had grown accustomed to, with each room housing approximately twenty girls. We found we would each have our own bunk and that we were even to be supplied with blankets. We also received a bowl, a cup and spoon and could only stare at one another, literally dumbfounded, because we no longer believed such luxuries were possible. But in the end, we were left with our empty dishes, waiting in vain for food to be served. It never arrived. Instead, an announcement came over a loudspeaker that there was a need for women with cooking experience, which started something of a stampede. Immediately, a large number of women began running from the barracks in answer to the call. I followed, more or less out of curiosity, and stood around outside the kitchen, observing this sudden flurry of activity.

Soon, four women were chosen to work in the inmates' kitchen and, as they assumed their chores, a high-ranking officer suddenly approached me and said, *"Du kleine, kommen Sie, kommen Sie!"* (You, little one, come, come.) His tone was not particularly menacing, but it had an urgent quality that startled me. As he grabbed my arm and led me toward another building, I began to regret my decision to stray so far from Magda. My curiosity, much like a cat's, might well be the death of me.

Along the way, the officer instructed yet another woman to come along with us, and I found this oddly reassuring. Once we had gone inside the second building, we were abruptly asked if we knew how to cook a good Hungarian goulash.

This question was so unexpected, so *preposterous* in life-threatening circumstances such as these, I had to fight the urge to laugh aloud. The other woman and I exchanged quizzical glances and then hastily assured the officer that we did *indeed* know how to make Hungarian goulash.

At this juncture, we were quickly led to the kitchen and given the necessary ingredients, including two hind legs of pork, to prepare a meal for forty German officers and personnel.

We discovered a pantry laden with a variety of good things to eat: salami, sugar, cases of jam, all sorts of delicacies that assailed the nostrils with their succulent aromas. We were under guard, of course, so could only feast upon these delicious morsels with our eyes. I hadn't realized what powers of restraint I possessed until I found myself in this extraordinary situation. Here, only a few feet away, was *food*—not the dirty, moldy garbage we were given each day, but beautifully fresh and nutritious food that tantalized the senses to the brink of madness! Still, I did not move from the spot where I stood. I looked at everything with great longing, but retained enough presence of mind to keep from leaping forward and gorging myself on the spot. My mind was working feverishly! There was *so much* here—enough to be shared with many other starving souls. We would have to devise a way to transport some of it back to the barracks. It was the life-giving sustenance that Magda needed, the only thing that could help insure that she would not soon again be selected for extermination. If I could build up that poor starving child with some of these wonderful foods, she would have a chance. As it was, I knew she would not long survive. Even if she were not again taken from the lines, I knew she would eventually expire on her own.

I worked with a furious diligence that night, inspired by a new purpose in life. I knew I was in a position to do much for myself and others if I went about it in the right way. I took as great pains to set the dining room tables attractively as I would have for a royal banquet. If everyone was pleased with the results, it could earn me a permanent place here and, if this was managed, then many other things could be managed as well.

As the goulash simmered slowly on the stove, my coworker and I became almost scientifically critical of the seasoning.

"Just another pinch of salt," I would tell her as I sampled it, and later, she would suggest I taste it again to see if it needed yet another clove of garlic. In this way, we were able to eat enough to satisfy our hunger without arousing the animosity of the guard. We were careful to avoid one another's eyes while this charade was going on, for we did not wish to trigger any spontaneous reactions. The tension of the moment had brought us dangerously close to impulsive behavior, and just then we were highly susceptible to fits of nervous laughter. But we managed to keep our composure, and later, were overjoyed when the meal was praised for its excellence.

That night, I managed to smuggle a few scraps

of food out of the kitchen and brought them back to the barracks, where I quickly fed them to Magda. The child was highly uncomfortable with what she felt to be a selfishly deceptive act and tried her best to swallow without chewing.

"Don't concern yourself," I told her in a low whisper. "We will gradually take care of the others as well. There is *so much food there,* Magda! More than you could possibly imagine. It will take some thought, but I will work out a way to get some of it back to the barracks."

"They will kill you if they find out!" Magda gasped in wide-eyed horror.

"Leave that to your mother," I retorted with an air of false bravado. "Now, look down there. You've dropped all those crumbs in your lap. Don't waste anything."

In the days that followed, our kitchen duties were gradually expanded. We received requests for homemade cakes and puddings, and since these were all recipes in which we excelled, we fell to the task with great enthusiasm.

I had always been proud of my pastries, and preparing them again reminded me of past holiday times, when life had revolved around family and friends, those precious loved ones who were with us no more. It was difficult to imagine what future celebrations might consist of—if we somehow managed to survive—with all the places at our table empty. I had never before thought of it in those terms, perhaps because I had not really counted on surviving, but now the awful fact came home to me. In the house where we had lived—or in any house in which we might *ever* live—we would have to exist with the ghosts of holidays past, and remember in our thoughts and dreams the lilt of children's laughter that would be no more, and the gaiety and singing that had always been part of our festive joy. Those members of our family who had blessed us with these expressions of love and good fellowship were gone. Now, there would only be empty chairs and painful memories, and whatever scraps of life one could salvage from that.

5

Had we had any contact with the outside world, we might have drawn some encouragement from the fact that by August 1944 the Russian summer offensives had brought the Red Army to the border of East Prussia. They had bottled up approximately fifty German divisions in the Baltic region, while a new attack on August 20 would result in the conquest of Romania by the end of the month, depriving the German armies of the Ploesti oil fields, their only major source of natural oil. Still, we would learn of German losses and retreats in other ways, because they were clearly reflected in the increased brutality of the Nazis toward their captives.

For a time—all too brief a time—life seemed to have taken on some degree of normalcy. Working in the kitchen was not an altogether unpleasant experience, although we were forbidden to share in the fruits of our labors. After the meals had been prepared, we were immediately relegated to the inmates' kitchen for our own supper. But we managed to consume a certain portion of what we cooked through the continued practice of "sampling," and while our German guard was not exactly naive, we were grateful that he preferred not to notice our periodic indulgences. This small laxness in the rules also encouraged me in my scheme to transport some of the food back to the barracks. I fell into the habit of hiding a pail of food in the pantry whenever I could, and later, after the dishes had been done and it had grown dark outside, I would sneak the pail back to the others. It was only a block or so but truly an interminable distance in a situation where detection meant certain death. As I moved along through that velvet darkness, it seemed that the very drumroll of my heart was enough to arouse the officers and bring them down upon me.

Once in the barracks, it became disheartening to distribute the food, since, of course, there was never enough for everyone. And then, too, there were not always opportunities to smuggle the pail out of the kitchen. The circumstances had to be just right, and they rarely were. Still, I managed to bring food back two or three times a week and worked out a kind of rotating system whereby everyone eventually received a taste of whatever I had stolen.

Over a period of time, I became deeply concerned with the welfare of two sisters who were close to Magda's age. I knew them as Terri and Irene, and the progression of their weakness had become more noticeable in recent days. Since they slept in nearby bunks I could see them actually deteriorating in front of my eyes and, as often as possible, would feed them whatever I could without appearing to slight the others. In the end, starvation affected us all the same, but a more heart-wrenching misery existed in watching the slow, painful decline of these young people. Parental instincts have a tendency to come forward at such times, and rightly or wrongly, take precedence over the needs of others. It was not difficult to give the youngsters more—in fact, it seemed only right.

As children would beg to hear fairy stories, I was repeatedly asked to describe the kitchen and the surrounding facilities in which I worked. I explained the way the pantry was laid out and itemized the foods found on each shelf.

"There is a large vegetable garden outside," I told them, "and there is some talk that we will also be working there before long. At the moment, they are installing a large gas-heated kettle, which I feel will have something to do with feeding the unfortunate victims confined to that makeshift hospital of theirs."

"How starved do you have to be before you are eligible to become a patient in their hospital?" one of the weaker girls asked snidely, without stirring from her bunk.

"Starvation is not an illness," another retorted quickly. "It is a fact of life. You will have to develop a disease more dramatic than that."

"I haven't the strength to develop something more dramatic than that," the girl answered listlessly, prompting a small round of laughter.

"Can you bring us some potatoes and turnips from the garden?" another girl asked then. "Or a nice, crisp green onion might be nice."

"That's enough!" Magda snapped suddenly. "Your endless requests are tiresome and altogether oblivious to the dangers involved. You act as if you need only make out a shopping list and my mother will bring back everything you want. Why don't you give a moment's thought to the fact that she risks her life over every scrap of food she smuggles in here."

"Well, that's never kept *you* from eating it," another of the girls observed coldly. "But then, of course, you have the best of it. After all, she always feeds you first. And the *most,* as far as that goes."

As Magda lunged toward the girl, I grabbed her by the hem of her skirt, and while this effectively restrained her, it also tore her uniform loose at the waist.

"Stop this!" I insisted then. "In a moment you will have the officers in here, and if that happens, hunger will be the least of our worries."

"Food is all they ever think about!" Magda persisted sullenly. "Well, from now on, they can have all of mine. I haven't any desire to magnify the importance of a few crumbs of food over that of a person's life. That's what we've all been doing in allowing you to continue this dangerous game, Mama. I'll have no more of it!"

"Spoken on a full stomach, no doubt," the first girl taunted and, since I was expecting Magda to retaliate as before, I was surprised to see her retire to her bunk and dissolve into tears. It was obvious she was deeply hurt and humiliated to think that others would actually accuse her of hoarding food. Knowing that the stubborn side of her nature could be aroused by such caustic remarks, I began to fear she might actually make good her threat to go on a hunger strike.

"Before any more commotion is created here," I said then, "I wish for all of you to know something. You are all the products of great pain and suffering, and have bravely endured many personal losses. In view of this, it would be impossible for me to judge you unkindly for your remarks. Still, I think you know you are all in my heart each day, and that what I want for my own child, I want for all of you. If it were possible, I would bring you the entire larder of that pantry rather than prepare another bite of anything for those evil ones who are responsible for our enslavement. But such wishes are not realistic. They are mere dreams, and painful ones at that, since they have no hope of ever coming true. So we must do what we can on the small pail of food I am able to bring back here. At least it is more than we had before, and thanks be to God for granting us a means of obtaining it."

I watched as the girl who had been taunting Magda now moved toward her and gently clasped her shoulder. Their eyes met, and I was relieved to see that there was no animosity in either glance.

It was a scene that was to be repeated many times. The pressures and anxieties of daily life caused periodic flare-ups, but they were counterbalanced by a unity of spirit that continued to prevail. To the extent that it was possible for us to feel concern and care for others, we did. We broke dry, stale pieces of bread into even smaller pieces and passed them around to those who had none. We shared scraps of food and drops of water as if they were pearls, attempting to appease our hunger pangs with the satisfaction found in small acts of compassion. It worked for me, as it did for many others, and if it was a delusion to believe that a giving heart was as rewarding as a full stomach, I doubt we were the worse for harboring such a belief.

Meanwhile, my kitchen duties continued, and as I had predicted, soon came to include a certain amount of work in the garden. By the end of the day, a highly discerning eye might have noticed that the contours of my figure had shifted slightly. They were frequently padded with a variety of raw vegetables which, despite my inadequate diet, gave me a certain lumpish appearance. When I arrived back at the barracks, the girls would devour the raw potatoes, turnips and greens just as they were, dirt and all. Water was a scarcity and could not be wasted on the cleansing of vegetables. Even had this been possible, it would have involved a certain amount of risk, and taking whatever risks were associated with the consumption of dirt seemed far the better bargain.

My own continued resistance to filth and disease came as no small surprise to me, for there was hardly any way to explain it. I had never been an exceptionally robust person, and yet now endured extreme heat and cold, starvation, pestilence and the cruelty of our captors with a new kind of resilience. It made me wonder how much of a person's good health was actually a matter of will. I knew that signs of infirmity were not tolerated here, and that survival depended upon remaining physically useful to the Reich. I had somehow managed to do that, and yet could not or *would* not accept the credit.

Always it seemed a higher power was guiding me, instructing me, aiding me in my efforts to preserve what was left of our lives, mine and Magda's. How else to explain the success of the many impulsive acts of a woman not normally given to impulse. Yet, at home, I had engaged in various black market activities and, since our incarceration, had twice stepped forward and snatched Magda from the lines marked for extermination. There was simply no reason in the world why I should still be around to wonder about it, and yet here I was. If I were being spared for a reason, it seemed vitally important to come to understand what that reason might be. It was too much to comprehend all in a moment, but I vowed to find the answer, and so this quest soon became the central theme of my life.

I became more aware of the suffering of others, which had the natural affect of diminishing my own. I no longer considered the risks involved in transporting food from the kitchen to the barracks. I assumed I had been chosen to perform this task because of certain innate qualities in myself that God had seen and I had overlooked. Except for this particular set of circumstances, I would never have come to recognize my own capabilities or potential, or even have reason to give a great deal of thought to either. There was no denying that ease and security in life had certain dulling effects. It brought to mind a humorous anecdote I had once heard, something that bordered on pitying the poor pedigreed dog inasmuch as he would never know the stimulus of fleas.

Well, we had known that and more, as well as things that should never have been known at all in the sense that they should never have happened. But history could not be altered, although history had altered us, and where we had once been proud individuals, we now stood at attention and saluted when the German soldiers came to inspect the kitchen.

On one such occasion, I had just popped a chunk of cabbage into my mouth and so could not properly address the officers when they spoke to me. One of them quickly noticed my discomfort—and the reason for it—and slapped me sharply on both cheeks, causing the cabbage to fly out of my mouth like a projectile. He was young and eager to prove himself, which would cause me some additional problems in the future, but I did not immediately understand that I had been selected by him as an object for personal surveillance.

It was never wise to relax our caution and, in situations where we did, there was always a price to be paid. In my own case, I learned my lesson at the hands of that same ambitious officer.

One day, a young girl came begging at the kitchen door and, soon after I had slipped her a raw onion, I was relieved of my duties in the kitchen.

Since I was preoccupied with the long-range ramifications of this—the loss of decent working conditions and the precious supply of extra food I had been taking back to the barracks—I did not immediately comprehend that there was yet another punishment in store for me.

"An example must be made of you!" the German officer said coldly. While I hadn't any notion of what he had in mind, the sardonic smile that crossed his face left me extremely unnerved.

"When we are finished with you, others will understand that rules were made to be obeyed and so will you! Nothing in that kitchen is to be given out to any mangy dog that passes. You were to see to the needs of the officers and personnel only. That is what you were told, but that is not what you have been doing. How very, very unfortunate."

It did not seem possible he could be this enraged over an incident involving one raw onion. I began to suspect he had somehow learned how I had been smuggling food back to the barracks, yet he never made any mention of it. As he pushed me along in front of him, he continued to rant and rave about the miserable wretches who actually had the audacity to come begging, and so I was forced to accept the fact that the onion alone was enough to cause whatever was to follow.

The young officer, intent upon being a credit to the Reich, ordered me to climb up on the chimney of a nearby bunker. I was given a large pail of water to hold in each hand and then was instructed to stand there for the balance of the day. He could not have devised a more inhumane form of punishment in that cold, wintry climate, and my limbs began turning numb and blue before I had even positioned myself according to his instructions. He then told me not to move, abruptly turned his back and quickly moved away.

And so began a grueling experience that seemed, even at the outset, beyond my capacity for endurance. Even without the weight of the water-filled pails, the bitter, frigid wind hammered and shrieked all around, threatening to dislodge my footing and pound me unconscious in the process. I stood slightly spread-legged to maintain my balance and tried to ignore the sharp, jabbing pains that assaulted my back and arms, although there was nothing else to think about. As my arms began to feel as if they were being torn from their sockets, the urge was strong to put down the pails, at least for a moment. But even without anyone about, I knew I was being closely observed and dared not risk such an impulsive act.

I decided I must not let my thoughts run wildly, that I must develop a more responsible and practical approach to this entire ordeal. I had an entire day to spend here. It could not be accomplished by trying to think hours ahead. I would have to think about getting through the next five minutes . . . and then another five . . . and another twenty until finally, a half-hour had passed. After that, the entire process would have to begin again, broken down into minutes and seconds and fractions of seconds in order to make it more endurable. The sky was gray and hazy, with only a suggestion of the sun. I tried to judge the time by its path, taking heart each time it appeared to have moved.

An *onion*! A single onion has caused all this, I thought. Hunger was everywhere. It was not to be condoned. Only in a world gone mad could such contradictions exist—and yet they did, and so did I. I existed amid all this madness and horror with an obsolete set of standards, the kind that perpetually attracted something bad from every attempt to do good. Since I could not begin to understand such a world, it was not the easiest thing to live in it, but I knew that I would have to try for Magda's sake. The girl continued to dominate my thoughts throughout the day as the sun slowly inched its way across the sky. At times, I only imagined its movement, but if I did not look at it too frequently, its progress became real, something that I could trust.

At long last, I saw a welcome sight in the distance. The girls were returning from the factory, which meant that the workday had ended. As they filed past, one glanced back more frequently than the rest. Although my vision had long since become blurred with the effects of constant, agonizing pain, I sensed it was Magda and prayed that she would not react impulsively and thus subject herself to a similar fate. I watched as an officer moved up beside her and prodded her along. After that, she risked only one more backward glance, and then slowly passed from view.

Pray for me, dear child! I thought, believing with all my heart in the strength of a child's prayers. If I did not survive this, I would not be permitted to survive at all, and I knew that I had to remain alive if only to know that Magda was alive.

As night began to fall, the officer who had become my personal tormentor suddenly passed before me. He did not stop or glance up in my direction. After he had passed several more times, I began to suspect he had actually forgotten I was out there in that bone-chilling night air.

And then, an extraordinary thing happened. As he passed before me one more time, a young girl suddenly raced up behind him and began pleading with him. She was a member of the office personnel—his secretary, I believe—and I listened curiously as she begged him to curtail my punishment.

"You have things to do," he reminded her curtly. "Leave me to my duties and tend to your own."

"I cannot bear it!" the girl wailed pathetically, and I saw then she was just a child, and hopelessly in love with this officer. "I can *see* her from where I sit at my desk. She shivers so, and I fear she may collapse. A-And the way she looks at me—her face haunts me in a way I can't explain!"

"You are a fool!" he spat and angrily pushed her away. "We have higher goals in life than that one! Concern yourself with the things that matter, the things that will make Germany victorious and supreme!"

"Please, Karl!" the girl persisted. "Take her down! It is dark now, and so cold! In the name of everything we have ever been to one another, *take her down!*"

He glanced at me angrily, uncomfortably, not certain how much German I understood. I met his eyes levelly, and saw the boy in him struggling to become a man.

"*All right then!* If it means getting some work done around here, I'll get her down," he grumbled and, under this pretext, I was finally allowed to come in from the cold.

"*Danke,*" I managed to say through lips rigid with cold and, as the girl nodded quickly, the officer shamefacedly looked away. I knew what they were thinking, that they had spared a human being, but in the process had failed their Fuehrer. It was all part of this ridiculous allegiance they had locked themselves into. But even as they looked for something to strive for, something to respect, to revere, to dedicate their lives to, they were beginning to realize this wasn't it. In time, they would have to face up to the consequences of their deeds and, even in my own particular circumstances, I could not imagine a fate more terrible than that.

When I returned to the barracks, I was immediately encircled by the girls who, along with my own hysterical child, helped me to my bunk. They barraged me with questions but soon realized I wasn't in any condition to answer. They briskly rubbed my hands and feet and covered me with their own bodies to provide some warmth. After a very long time, I began to respond to their ministrations. When they saw my condition was somewhat improved, they once again began to question me.

"What happened, Mama? Why did they punish you like that? You were only cooking for them!"

I explained what had happened, hastening to add that what had occurred had been basically my own fault.

"Things were going so well for a while that it lured me into a false sense of security. I should have realized that this particular officer was seeking to elevate his position through me. I know it now. I'm afraid I haven't anything for you to eat tonight. My carelessness has brought an end to that."

As I lay back down in my bunk, I stared up into gaunt, hungry faces that insisted I had nothing to apologize for, and so came to realize that in this war between major nations, we had somehow managed to become an army in our own right.

By the end of August, the German armies in the West had lost 500,000 men and almost all of their tanks, artillery and trucks. With so little to defend the Fatherland, most of the German generals in that area began to feel the end had come. But Hitler had other ideas, and continued to prod them on with his own extraordinary promises and dreams.

"If necessary," he told them, "we'll fight on the Rhine. It doesn't make any difference. Under all circumstances, we will continue this battle until, as Frederick the Great said, one of our damned enemies gets too tired to fight any more. We'll fight until we get a peace which secures the life of the German nation for the next fifty or a hundred years and which, above all, does not besmirch our honor a second time, as happened in 1918. . . . I live only for the purpose of leading this fight because I know that if there is not an iron will behind it, this battle cannot be won."

The result of Hitler's own iron will caused new policies to be enforced in the recruitment of additional armies. Boys between the ages of fifteen and eighteen were called, as were men between the ages of fifty and sixty. During September and October 1944, another half-million men were enlisted, causing severe shortages of manpower in both factories and offices.

A variety of exhortations went out to these new draftees of the Western Front, urging them to defend Germany's sacred soil to the very last, and forbidding them to give up a square foot of German soil without a fight. It was all great bravado but did not prevent an increasing number of desertions by those who no longer believed in the cause. A proclamation was soon issued to counteract such activities and advised in part that

> every deserter . . . will find his just punishment. Furthermore, his ignominious behavior will entail the most severe consequences for his family. . . . They will be summarily shot.

As war activities became more highly accelerated, it forced a change in our daily routine at the camp, which was known as Branow Lager 15, Camp 15 and was located near Bromberg (now Bydgoszcz), Poland. I could no longer be wasted on the menial tasks I had been assigned to. Since my experience on the bunker, I had been removed from the kitchen to collect the human waste out of the latrines and spread it on the gardens. In being reduced to this task, I was made to understand I was considered no better than the foul stuff I had to work with, and was frequently reminded of this fact. But suddenly, my services became more valuable to the Reich, and I was sent to work in a factory, assigned to the same Commando where my daughter worked.

The factory was approximately six kilometers from camp, situated in a large forest, framed by tall, ancient trees. The letters N.G.L. had been printed on the front of the building, which was painted a dark forest green to effectively camouflage its existence.

Once inside, I saw it was an ammunition plant. I was assigned to load huge sacks of fire bomb powder into waiting trucks. Each shift was ten hours long and, during one such period, I loaded 1,800 bags of powder unassisted. At the end of that time, I had stabbing pains in my sides and back and could barely breathe.

The weight of the powder and the weight of survival seemed to be the same. I felt that both were becoming a burden beyond my endurance and could only hope I might eventually be assigned to another task.

That night, in the barracks, Magda became the protective and consoling one, stroking my brow and offering what moral support she could.

"It isn't fair," she said, in a soft, crooning tone. "You are so good, so selfless and caring. They haven't any right to treat you this way. I've seen the way it is, Mama. They assign the hardest duties to the Jewish women. A lot of the Polish and Russian girls are being paid for their services, and they all have easier jobs and better food to eat. It simply isn't fair!"

I had to smile at the youthful quality in her that still sought the fairness in things. After all this, she expected some rhyme or reason for the way things were.

The next day, I was assigned to a task that could not be said to be any improvement over what I had been doing. I was required to help unload a trainful of iron barrels which weighed about 100 kilograms each.

We were performing these tasks on a daily diet of watery soup and a slice of bread with margarine. Although the allotted ration of soup was to have been three-fourths of a liter, it was seldom more than one-half. In any case, it was totally inadequate to our needs. Now, I often indulged myself in fond memories of that aromatic pantry I would see no more, and the bountiful vegetable garden outside. In retrospect, it seemed I had once enjoyed a luxurious existence there, although I sensed that this was just my mind playing tricks on me.

As the war effort continued, the hard, cold winter came, severely compounding our physical distress. Although I was more frequently chosen for indoor jobs than any other kind, Magda was less fortunate. She continued to work outside, loading wagons with another girl, without benefit of winter clothing.

When the workday ended, our agony was prolonged by the damnable roll call, which was never expedited because of rain, sleet or snow. In every instance, we were at the mercy of the whims of our commandant, who might suddenly decide we should scrub down the barracks before retiring for the night.

As the Germans stopped suffering defeats and began to suffer mass annihilations, the cruelty at the camps became more pronounced. The way we made our beds was suddenly an issue of great importance. Every crease and fold was examined for perfection and, since perfection was rarely achieved, the girls who had not made their beds exactly right were cursed and beaten as if they had committed some major act of sabotage.

In marching back and forth from the factory to the camp, the officer in charge of our group suddenly developed a tyrannical quality we had not seen earlier. She, like many of the women officers, was given to more brutal disciplinary actions than her male counterparts, and now began to openly criticize the uneven formation of our lines.

"Hold your lines! Hold your lines!" she would scream in her harsh, shrill voice, slapping and pushing the girls in the outside lines to encourage better symmetry. How absurd it all was, as if we were on parade before royalty and not merely trudging through this remote forest, a ragged, tired army of no immediate interest or concern to anyone except this one officer. She always walked with a huge German Shepherd who had been taught to attack upon command. As the days went along, these commands came more frequently, and it was a gruesome sight to see the soft, powdery snow suddenly beaded with the blood of some poor unfortunate girl who could not avoid the eager jaws of the dog. As the dog bared its teeth and snarled and the girl screamed, the German officer would laugh uproariously, as if it were all great sport. No matter how the victim might be mutilated that day, it never excused her from her duties. While we would attempt to assist her as inconspicuously as possible, we were rarely successful in our attempts.

Despite our efforts to remain optimistic—made easier now by occasional reports that things weren't going so well for the Germans—our overall mood was one of total desolation. The backbreaking work and meager diet were taking their toll, and we no longer cared if the officers saw us at work with tears streaming down our cheeks.

After we returned to the barracks, we would go around by the kitchen and sift through the garbage, looking for potato peelings or anything else edible.

"It is senseless to go on in this way," I told Magda one night. "The only thing that can improve our situation now is to find a way of providing those cooks with something they cannot get any other way. if I can think of something, I suspect they will be ready to trade us some food for it."

"Oh Mama, you are dreaming," Magda replied with a heavy sigh. "Or else you've grown delirious with hunger. You are starting to talk the way you did back home when you had some means of obtaining soap and nice fabrics, but there is nothing here, only what you see. So, we'll eat garbage and be satisfied with it."

But I found I could no longer be satisfied with it, because if we were to continue working at the pace expected of us, we would simply have to have better food.

With a heightened sense of perception, I began to look about my work area each day, trying to envision how *this* thing might be made out of *that* thing. Before long, I noticed that the powder we were working with was contained in rubberized nylon bags. As the glimmer of an idea began to form, I stole one of the bags from the pile and quickly retreated into the bathroom. There I wound it around my body under my dress, and in this way, managed to bring it back to the barracks with me. That night I sat and painstakingly peeled the rubber away, leaving a nice piece of nylon fabric. At this point, I approached one of the cooks in the kitchen and told her I would make her a nice brassiere if she could manage to get me a needle, a scissors and some buttons to work with. Since the cook was in daily contact with a number of civilians who delivered groceries to the kitchen, she promptly managed this. Before long, she had her brassiere, and I had some boiled potatoes and bread.

This bit of ingenuity led to orders for additional brassieres from the other cooks and some of the office girls. Of course, I was eager to fill their requests and only wished I might have had the proper tools to work with. As it was, I worked by candlelight after everyone had gone to sleep and unraveled long nylon threads from the bags to have something to sew with. The material was coarse and stiff and my fingers bled profusely from pushing the needle through the fabric without the aid of a thimble. It was a slow, awkward procedure, but afforded a few extra potatoes that could be fed to my child and the two sisters, Terri and Irene, and so was well worth the effort.

I had learned to sew at a very young age and was already making dresses by the time I was thirteen. It was a fortunate education that was proving invaluable to me now, and I knew I would continue to capitalize on it for as long as I was able to obtain the nylon bags.

In time, I was asked by the office girls if I could supply them with garter belts to hold up their stockings. I tried to remember what it was like to even *have* stockings because, despite the wintry weather, we were forced to work with bare feet shoved into ill-fitting canvas shoes with hard, wooden soles. Still, this did not seem to be the time to become steeped in envy or self-pity. Additional orders meant additional food, and so my clandestine activities continued.

The long nights spent crouched in one corner of my bunk with my nylon bags and a few sewing supplies were fruitful ones, although they made the next day's labors even more exhausting than they already were.

"Mama, you can't keep this up," Magda insisted one evening after I had been repeatedly scolded by the factory foreman for failing to meet my production quota. "You were lucky today. They only badgered you about it. Tomorrow, they will begin to suspect something and, if you continue to fall behind, you know what will happen."

"We are constantly living on the brink of something happening, precious child. It is futile to consider that at every turn. We have others to think of besides ourselves. You have become extremely fond of Terri and Irene and know the extra provisions that come from the cooks are as vital to their survival as to ours. A little ingenuity can carry us a long way. You will find this is true in all walks of life, not only during wartime. That is how your father and I succeeded in business, and it is the only way you can achieve any worthwhile goal. You must dare to achieve, Magda, not always be afraid of your own courage and daring. These qualities were given to you for a reason. You can readily see the difference they can make in a person's circumstances. At the moment, the difference is only a matter of a few potatoes, but they are important to us, are they not? If we have them and others go without, we have earned the right to them. So it is in everything. What you have earned in life is not necessarily what you can afford to buy. You earn only those things you expend some effort for. If God had not intended for us to apply our imagination and ingenuity to things, he would not have given us those traits."

Magda had grown curiously silent and reflective as I spoke, trying to evaluate my side of the argument as objectively as she could. In recent months, I had often assailed her ears with similar complex points of view, ignoring her age and inexperience. But I did not know how much time we had, or if we were even destined to go on together, and this constant uncertainty compelled me to give her an abbreviated rendition of life, according to my own perception of it. I wished, as all parents do, for her to benefit from my advice and learn from my mistakes so that she would not repeat them. I realized then that I no longer spoke to her or treated her as a child. With no time for frivolous thoughts or actions, I had been forced to cancel out her childhood and now expected her to think and behave as an adult. Insofar as she was capable of living up to my expectations, she sincerely attempted to do so. I watched her vacillate daily between the role of a girl and that of a woman, trying her best to find the proper way to act and the right person to be. There could be no doubt she had lost a quality of youth and innocence that could never be recaptured. The events of the recent past had forced all of these girls into a sudden maturity that was indeed sad to behold.

It brought to mind a curious fact that continued to haunt me, dating back to our original journey to Auschwitz. Having been packed into that suffocating cattle train like so many dead or dying animals, I had cradled Magda's small sister, Lillian, in my arms, attempting as best I could to protect her from harm. It would have been understandable if the child had been overcome by hysteria and behaved wildly and uncontrollably as many of the adults did. But she had lain quietly in my arms, gazing up at me with a kind of solemn resignation. Since that time, I had often dreamed of that tiny little face which reflected such calm and composure in the midst of all that chaos. Her behavior had not been typical of a baby, and could not be explained in any logical way. While it was inconceivable that she could have known what lay ahead, she had behaved on this one occasion as if she understood the futility of struggle. Veronica, too, had stood quietly by my side, her fingers clutching the hem of my coat until the decision was made for her to be taken from me. Then, when the order was given, she had obediently gone with Bertha without even a trace of childish rebellion.

Had the two younger children survived, I knew they would have been as drastically altered by our experiences as Magda had been. Whatever attitudes and ideas Magda would eventually assume would no longer be the product of her upbringing. All that had been eradicated by this time of horror and suffering. When it was over, it would be *this* time she would remember, not happy childhood experiences, and not the comfort and security of home. The past had been stripped away and could never be reclaimed in the sense that we had known it.

The only reality now was a life not worth living, an existence no better than that of animals in a cage. We were starved and punished, and starved and punished some more.

The factory foreman was an elderly Pole whose anti-Semitic beliefs made life all the more difficult for us. He had a habit of harassing any worker who paused for even a moment while on the job, insisting that there wasn't any time for idleness.

On one occasion, when he reported us to a German soldier close at hand, the German turned to him and said, "Why don't you give those poor unfortunate girls a chance to catch their breath?" The Pole was amazed at this reaction, just as we were, although we occasionally saw some display of sympathy from the German soldiers. To the extent that it was shown, it deserves some acknowledgment.

Another time, when we were being transported on the cattle train to the camp in Poland, a German soldier who had noticed Magda lying curled up on the floor of the car, gave in to an impulsive gesture of compassion and covered her with his own coat. Such acts were a welcome respite from the harsh cruelty of the SS officers but, of course, were few and far between.

As the bitter winter advanced, our suffering and despair became more pronounced. Forced to work outdoors without sweaters or coats, we walked about in deep snow in our wooden-soled shoes, wishing we might have had some stockings or warm socks as well.

Many succumbed to the elements and were envied by the rest of us for having escaped the fate we were still forced to endure. Whatever news we heard concerning the war had little effect on us—even if the information was optimistic. We were only conscious of hunger and bone-chilling cold, a never-ending cycle of agonizing pain which was relentless in its quest to destroy us all.

Meanwhile, Adolph Hitler was engaged in his last desperate gamble to launch a mighty offensive in the West. This daring plan was intended to take the Allies by surprise and overpower them before they had a chance to recover. It was a military tactic that did not take into account that the German Army had grown much weaker than it was in 1940, and that it was now pitted against a far more resourceful enemy.

But despite the odds, Hitler was determined to regain the initiative by splitting the U.S. Third and First armies, and by advancing to Antwerp and depriving General Eisenhower of his main port of supply. Once he had freed himself of the threat to Germany's western border, he hoped to turn against the Russians, who were still advancing in the Baltics.

During November 1944, Hitler managed to assemble nearly 2,500 new or rebuilt tanks and assault guns and in December another 1,000. It amounted to scraping the bottom of the barrel, although he did not choose to think of it in those terms.

The generals who came to the Fuehrer's headquarters at Ziegenberg for a briefing could not ignore the fact that they were in the company of a sick and desperate man. A palsylike trembling had attacked his hands and, when he walked, he dragged one foot behind him. But his fiery spirit prevailed, enabling him to convince his reluctant generals that his desperate plan had some merit, and once again, they came away with the determination to carry out his orders as best they could.

6

In mid-December, a shipment of winter clothing arrived at the camp and, while we had hoped that these garments might be composed of something more substantial, they were only long-sleeved dresses made out of a flannel-like striped material. In such freezing temperatures, they did not provide much additional protection, and so our casualties continued to mount.

But the Germans hadn't any regard for such losses. They had now become totally preoccupied with sparing themselves. Almost daily, we were subjected to the activities associated with an air raid, forced to go into hiding until the bombers had passed, although they never bombed the camp or the forest in which the factory was located.

Meanwhile, we continued to produce the ammunition that would be responsible for killing our relatives and friends, and often hoped that a bomb would land right in our midst so that the whole miserable business would finally be over with.

Then, in January of 1945, we began to feel that something was about to happen because all the factories cut back on production due to a shortage of raw materials. We had hoped this might mean, among other things, we could return to the shelter of the barracks where we would be allowed to wait out the balance of the war. But this was not to be, since we were looked upon as a work force that had to be utilized until the proverbial last dog was hung.

We were taken out to another section of the forest where we were told to gather firewood. The logs were buried under a thick blanket of snow, and we dug for them until our hands were numb and blue. As we stacked the wood in neat piles, we saw that the Gestapo officers had built several bonfires for their own comfort and that of their German Shepherd dogs. But although we gazed at these fires longingly, we were never allowed to get close enough to enjoy even a suggestion of their soothing warmth.

Severe cold, like severe hunger, is an all-consuming experience. As the numbness overtook our bodies, we prayed it might afford some relief from the elements, but it only made it that much harder to function. Our fingers refused to bend, our limbs moved awkwardly and lethargically, ignoring our wishes. Four times I sought to lift the same log from the snow, and each time it slipped from my fingers and fell to the ground again. The neat piles we had been instructed to assemble teetered precariously as our clumsy, frozen bodies collided with them. When the logs began to shift and roll back to the ground, the wrath of the German officers became almost maniacal. We were ordered to reconstruct the wood piles immediately, although speed was impossible in this frozen world. In time, it became an agonizing effort to move at all. Each painful step made us feel that our brittle bones would surely snap from the cold.

As the officers and their dogs lounged around the fires, we formed small circles and danced about in a frantic effort to kindle some circulation. I felt at times that we were performing a kind of ritualistic Dance of Death, although we sang a Hungarian song that spoke of survival and freedom.

> Up with your heads, Jewish girls. Our day will come when we will be free again.

Had the guards understood or concerned themselves with the message of our song, they would undoubtedly have silenced us, because we were only allowed to sing patriotic German songs that glorified them on our marches to and from work.

After a few moments of this agitated activity, we returned to work and, each time we did, our numbers were less. Those who fell by the wayside were soon obliterated from view by the falling snow. No effort was made to revive them or to keep them alive. As time went on, we frequently clawed at a mound of snow which turned out to be one of our comrades rather than the wooden log we thought it was.

Magda appeared as close to collapse as I had ever seen her. She moved in a slow, robotic manner, performing her duties with no real awareness of her actions. What few words I managed to say to her seemed to have no effect. It occurred to me that she might not have heard me, since the dense, deep snow had muffled all the sounds around us. It was like talking through thick walls of cotton; perhaps in the end, we would all simply drown in this thick, mesmerizing silence.

As I tugged at her arm, Magda turned toward me, and only then did I catch the words she was muttering under her breath. "I fear I cannot make it, Papa. If you are still alive, I doubt I will see you again."

It had not occurred to me that she still held out any real hope of seeing her father again, but I should have known she would cling to this possibility to have yet another reason to keep going. It was a game we all played: I must live for this person, for that person, for something, for *anything*! It was our way of buying enough courage for another day, another hour, another moment.

As my icy fingers clutched Magda's in a vain attempt to warm them, I tried to reassure her before the guards took notice of us.

"If Papa is alive, you will see him again. Listen to the artillery in the distance. Each day it comes closer. The Americans and Russians are beating the Germans back. You can tell that from the way these officers behave. There is still hope for us."

"They cannot come in time," Magda responded in a low, disconsolate tone. "Not for me. If you knew how I felt inside, Mama, you would know it is too late for me."

For the first time since we had been taken by the Germans, she seemed totally detached from me. I no longer felt that anything I said or did would make much difference, and this frightened me more than everything that had happened thus far.

As the day progressed, I occasionally lost track of her. Although I did my best to keep her in my field of vision, this was not always possible. Finally, after a very long time, I found her behind a tree, curled up in a pathetic little ball, sobbing her heart out. I realized then that the reason for her periodic disappearances had been to conceal her misery from me. Starvation and intense cold were taking their toll on her, but her primary fear was that I might know—as if I did not know already.

As I moved toward her, she anxiously whirled about, then jumped to her feet and attempted to look productive. It was a pathetic attempt at best, but I let her believe she had fooled me, because then she had a purpose: to keep me deluded about the extent of her despair.

At the close of each day, we were required to bring back the bodies of those who had not survived the pace and the elements. Dead or alive, we all had to report for roll call.

On the surface, the New Year held out small promise for those of us who were still around to bear the brunt of the cruel acts expended daily by the camp's German officers. As the artillery fire thundered on, it seemed to incite the most barbaric and bizarre behavior in our captors.

Had we known more than we did, we might have understood the reason for this. On January 12, 1945, Russia launched its greatest offensive of the war. Stalin had dispatched 180 divisions, many of them armored, into Poland and East Prussia alone. It had become an all-out onslaught that refused to be stopped. By the end of January, Hitler had begun receiving memoranda from many of his key people, warning that the war was lost. One such report came from Albert Speer, his Minister for Armament and War Production. Speer pointed out that there was only a two-week supply of coal for the German railways, power plants and factories and, since the Silesian industrial basin was now lost, he could only supply one-quarter of the coal and one-sixth of the steel Germany had been producing in 1944. This, he said, guaranteed certain defeat in 1945.

Still, Hitler chose to ignore the logic in this totally objective report. In truth, he barely glanced at it, dismissing Speer as someone who always seemed to have something unpleasant to say.

And so it was that during that period, while the leaders of the Reich began to pin their hopes on extremely slender threads, the reality of the situation became known to a greater number of German troops, who chose to react in both hysterical and heinous ways.

In our own camp, we noticed that the Germans had begun to run about like crazy people. The commandant in charge of the camp's operation developed the ruthless violence of a wild animal; like a vulture in a tree, he waited to swoop down upon any poor soul who had committed a minor infraction. The punishment was always totally out of proportion to the crime, and so we quickly became dedicated to the single objective of avoiding the malicious wrath of this obviously unbalanced individual.

"I think they must all have gone insane with their own guilt," Magda remarked one evening. "What else could cause them to act this way?"

"How about the loss of the war?" another girl suggested hopefully.

This was a possibility we now entertained daily, although it was rarely discussed. We had become superstitious enough to believe that if we dared to speak of such a miracle, it might never happen. So, even as this thought burned in everyone's minds, we spoke of other things and, in the process, Magda and I learned something more of the backgrounds of the sisters, Terri and Irene.

Like ourselves, the girls had once lived in a small Czechoslovakian community, Vilok by name, with a population of approximately 4,000. A fourth of Vilok's residents had been Jewish. Terri and Irene had entered Auschwitz with their mother, their 85-year-old paternal grandmother, an aunt and her three children, and an uncle with four children. (None of these unfortunate relations survived the gas chambers. After the war was over, only one uncle, who had been sent to a forced labor camp, would return as a surviving family member.)

As we sadly reflected upon their losses—and our own—we suddenly received an order to roll up our blankets, place them on our shoulders, and then line up at the front gate of the camp.

Since it was Sunday, we found this command a curious one, but quickly did as we were told. After the counting process was completed, we each received a piece of stale bread to take along. The food supply had been dwindling in recent days, and finally the deliveries stopped altogether. We knew instinctively that we were being readied for another journey. While no mention was made of where we were being taken or why, with the relentless approach of the Russians the *why* was altogether obvious.

There originally had been 1,000 women in our camp. Now, there were only 600, and to this figure were added the patients in the hospital, or

Revere as it was known, and some prisoners from another camp close by.

The hospital patients were loaded onto sleds, which we were required to pull with us as we marched off in a direction totally opposite that of the factory.

We saw at once that the roads were crowded with soldiers and civilians who were fleeing in every direction, seeking to spare their own lives. Many families were traveling in horse-drawn wagons, and there were also some trucks and cars on the road, as well as people on horseback. Despite a heavy blanket of new snow, the paths were already blackened by this incessantly heavy traffic.

The thick, white powdery stuff clung stubbornly to our wooden-soled shoes, weighing us down and making our progress extremely slow and agonizing. Pulling the sleds behind us impeded us even more, causing the German officers to scream at us to hurry along. It seemed it was always my personal misfortune to fall under the immediate jurisdiction of one of the women officers, and now once again I saw one of them running up behind me to strike me across the shoulders with a long stick. I would never forget that day, for it seemed endless and fraught with uncertainty and fear concerning our ultimate destination. Every time we were moved, it always forced us to consider the most extreme consequences. Since we were never enlightened as to our destination, it was easy enough to assume that we had been marked for death.

We passed through the city of Bromberg that day, and found it nearly deserted except for a handful of Germans who were themselves executing a hasty retreat. Some time later, we reached a forest where we were allowed to rest for five minutes, although we were warned not to eat up all of our bread since it was impossible to say how many more days we would still have to walk.

After our brief rest, we continued walking on and on until nightfall, and then for several hours afterward. The cold wind burned our faces and seared our lungs, while our bodies perspired profusely from our daylong physical exertion.

And then, almost like a mirage in the light of the full moon, I noticed a farmhouse up ahead. It was the most inviting scene I had ever beheld, suggesting our long-lost comforts of hearth and home.

"When we get to that farm," I whispered to Magda, "we will make our escape. I cannot walk any farther."

Magda was horrified at this suggestion. "Oh no, Mama! You mustn't consider such a risky idea. Not now! I know you are tired, but if we remain with the group, in a few more days we may be free."

I was not inclined to agree, but could not deny that my sudden decision had been prompted by an overwhelming wave of fatigue. Perhaps she was right after all. Such reckless, impulsive behavior might easily cost us our lives and, with the

Russians so close at hand, it seemed logical to let them resolve matters through a normal course of events, rather than making hasty and poorly conceived decisions of my own.

I nodded with silent resignation and continued to plod along with the others, until at last we came to another large farm, where we were abruptly herded into a large barn.

As large as it was, the barn was too small to comfortably accommodate our numbers and, once the doors had been closed and padlocked from the outside, I felt certain I knew our fate.

"Children, we have come to the end of our journey," I said, somewhat prophetically. "Now that they have locked us in here, they are sure to burn down the barn."

There immediately ensued the general clamor that one might expect with such a pronouncement, but I myself felt strangely calm. We had fought long and hard, and had come as far as we could go. My own state of exhaustion made any further efforts to survive both impossible and somewhat ludicrous. It occurred to me then that I should not have let Magda dissuade me when I suggested abandoning the rest of the group, but now it was too late to bemoan that choice. It made no more sense than blaming my mother for her unfortunate reluctance to follow my father to America. We had all made our share of bad decisions along the way and, in life, depending upon which door you went through, you were obliged to get whatever was on the other side.

As I lay down on a small pile of rough straw, Magda inched in and attempted to lie down beside me. This was not easily accomplished, because 900 people crowded into a barn does not leave much room for anything.

We lay there and listened to the others complain that someone was stepping on their foot, their arm or their head. At one point, a voice loudly protested that someone was urinating on them, and so it went.

Outside, the Gestapo officers shot their rifles into the air each time the bedlam inside the barn began to tax their patience.

With senses that had become extremely sensitive to the threat of imminent danger, I sniffed the air for the first suggestion of smoke and, as best I could, listened for sounds of suspicious movements outside.

"Are we going to die, Mama?" Magda asked, with a curious calm.

"It is their chance to rid themselves of all of us without wasting any of their precious ammunition," I reasoned. "I would be surprised if they did not avail themselves of such an opportunity."

"But maybe—"

"Hush, my child. Don't try to think anymore. What will be will be. Try to get some rest. If I am wrong about this, you will need all of your strength tomorrow."

It did not seem to me that we slept, yet there

were certain lapses in consciousness that could not be explained any other way. I would find myself suddenly aroused by some unusual noise in the barn and sense that some time had passed. In this way, the moments and the hours crept by, and finally it was morning, a morning that in some respects was the most beautiful I had ever seen, since I had not expected to see it at all.

When at last the barn doors were opened, we were ordered to line up outside, and clumsily stumbled out into the sunlight, covered with dirt and straw, barely able to move our cramped limbs.

As the counting procedure got under way, we could only hope that some mention would soon be made of food or water, but the only word we finally received was the familiar order to march.

The turmoil in the streets was twice what it had been the previous day. Everywhere one looked, there were German soldiers running from the Russians, as this tenacious army closed in for the kill. They were so close now that the ground actually shook beneath us with each report of artillery or machine gun fire. It was not unlike trying to move through an earthquake. After about two hours, we noticed that the officers in charge of our group had begun to behave erratically, running far ahead of us with the single-minded intent of saving their own skins.

"This is it!" I told Magda. "We won't go any farther." With that, I sat down by the side of the road. Immediately, Magda and a small group of girls flocked around, urging me to come along.

"The streets are full of German soldiers!" they warned. "They will shoot you if you do not obey."

"They won't bother us anymore," I replied confidently. "They are too concerned with saving themselves."

The immediate state of chaos seemed to bear this out, for no one gave us a glance as German soldiers and civilians alike continued to hurry past in their directionless frenzy.

After a few moments, the group of girls moved away from Magda and me, although they continued to look back apprehensively. As they slowly faded from sight, we remained where we were, determined to survive or perish on our own.

Shari Weisberger (now Shirley Lebovitz), 1946

Magda Weisberger, 1946

Solomon Weisberger in his Czech army uniform. He perished near Wels, Austria.

Shari with daughters Magda and Veronica beside the porch of their home, 1940. Veronica perished at Auschwitz.

Shari with Magda and Veronica, 1941

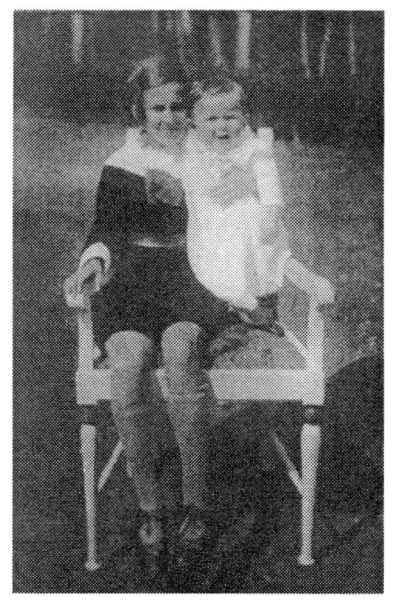

Magda and Baby Lillian, 1942. Lillian perished at Auschwitz.

Margaret Kraus, who perished at Aushwitz

Margaret's son, Joseph Kraus, who escaped from the camps and also eventually came to the United States to live

Bertha Weisberger, who perished at Auschwitz

Manny Lebovitz

Shari Weisberger's family, in 1932, clockwise from right to left: father Isidor Klein, Magda Weisberger, mother Gitl Klein, sister Blanche Klein, brother David Klein, Shari Klein Weisberger. Center: brother Adolph Klein, who drowned.

Ernest Willinger, Magda Willinger and Shirley Lebovitz at the KZ Friedhof Cemetery, in Wels, Austria, June 1990

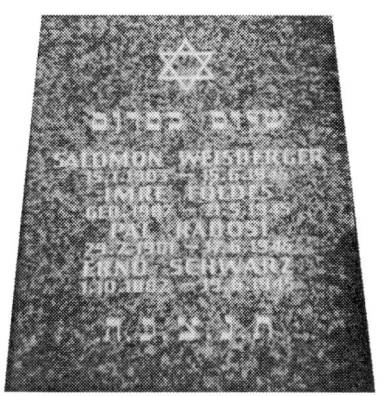

The gravestone of Solomon Weisberger, Imre Foldes, Pal Radosi, Ernö Schwarz, erected 1990

7

Since freedom had been our only thought for such a very long time, we had not stopped to consider what it might entail. Now, as we thought of the possible consequences for the first time, we began to see danger in every corner.

Moving along the streets as unobtrusively as possible, we avoided direct eye contact with the German soldiers, hoping in some way to remain invisible to them.

In the distance, I could see black smoke pouring from the chimney of a small farmhouse and concluded that it was as logical a destination as any. Pointing it out to Magda, I told her we would head in that direction and pray for a friendly reception.

I could see that the child had been strongly affected by the girls who had warned us about deserting the line. She moved along stealthily beside me, not altogether certain we had made the right decision.

"Come along," I told her gently. "We have already lost everything of any importance, including every shred of human dignity. Perhaps it is time to recapture a little of that."

I watched her straighten her shoulders then, abandoning for the first time the cowering stature that had become second nature to us all.

We walked through snow-covered fields and bitter cold toward that farmhouse in the distance, often stumbling and falling into ditches along the way.

When at last we reached the farm, we rapped softly on the door, and our knock was immediately answered by a diminutive old Polish woman who cordially invited us in.

There is no way to express what we felt in finally entering a structure that represented something more civilized and hospitable than just another compound. To see large, comfortable pieces of furniture, rugs on the floor and curtains at the windows was a sight almost too wondrous to behold. Our overpowering delight in seeing these things made us momentarily oblivious to the group of German soldiers seated around a large table. But when at last we recognized the uniforms, and those all-too-familiar militant faces, we were once again reduced to a state of total panic. Since we so obviously looked like refugees from a concentration camp, it would have been pointless to pretend we were anything else. Had we had some decent clothes and an opportunity to clean up, we might have been able to disguise ourselves, but as it was, we were once again at the mercy of the Germans.

With a sharp intake of breath, we waited for the inevitable, but then began to notice that these officers were carelessly sprawled about, with their uniforms open at the throat and strangely devoid of the menacing qualities we had always associated with them. Their eyes flickered over us indifferently and then returned to the food and drink that had been prepared for them.

I glanced at Magda, who seemed to have turned to stone, and gently nudged her into one corner of the room. There, we sank down to the floor near a wood-burning stove, reveling in the comfort of its soothing warmth after so many months in the bitter cold. The Polish woman asked us who we were, and I answered her honestly.

"Jewish girls from the concentration camp. We were originally from Czechoslovakia—or Hungary, as it has been known at times. I'm not sure who will control it now."

"Have you had anything to eat?" she asked politely.

"Not in several days. But we don't wish to impose."

"We can manage," she said sympathetically, and I knew then that while her own food supplies were limited, she would indeed manage, for that was her way. A few moments later, she brought us some hot tea, bread and butter, and tears of gratitude prevented us from thanking her properly.

After a time, we became fairly accustomed to the constant stream of traffic that passed through the house and the sight of the German uniforms did not alarm us as much as before. Those who stopped did so mainly to warm up before moving on their way. By evening, the faces had changed many times and it began to occur to us that we were overstaying our welcome.

"Everyone else is coming and going, Mama," Magda said self-consciously. "Perhaps it is time we left."

"Wait a moment," I told her. "Let me speak with the woman of the house and see what I can arrange."

When I found the right opportunity, I pulled the Polish woman aside and quickly explained our situation. "Both my daughter and I are totally exhausted from many days and nights of endless walking. If you would consider letting us stay for a few days, I would be most appreciative. I haven't any money to offer you, but we have these blankets which are quite nice, and you are certainly welcome to them."

"Of course you may stay," she said at once, "but as crowded as it is, I fear there is nowhere for you to sleep except on the floor."

"Oh God, it is a luxury to us! It is so warm and comfortable here. If you only knew what—" I found I could go no further. As the entire experience flashed before my eyes, I knew there was no way to explain it all in a moment. Overcome with emotion, I hugged and kissed the Polish woman, which encouraged Magda to do the same. Then, we went back to our corner and settled down for the night.

"It is too good to be true!" Magda said, echoing my own thoughts. "The lady has three daughters. I met them all and they are very nice. They have several head of cattle and some milk cows on this farm. Perhaps we could help them with their chores and—"

"No, sweet child. You must not let yourself grow attached to this place. The lady is already overextending herself in allowing us to stay on. We cannot take advantage of her generosity."

"But there is so much to be done here! We could help her in a thousand ways. I am sure that if we were to make ourselves useful. . . . "

For a time I listened to her prattle on, understanding all too well her overzealous determination to remain in this nucleus of peace and relative comfort. In that moment, I felt much as she did, but even as one part of me longed to stay there forever, another part was compelled to find its way back home, to whatever still remained of those things we had left behind.

Perhaps, through some miracle, others had also survived. I had to know! Their survival—or demise—had to be confirmed. No further plans could be made until I knew.

Patiently, I explained to Magda the need to get back to our roots and the shattered remnants of our past.

"That is the only thing we can rightfully build upon. We do not belong here. These people have their own lives to lead."

All through the night, the constant stream of soldiers and civilians continued. In the morning, six girls from our camp arrived and remained with us while we were there. They could hardly believe it when some of the German soldiers in the house offered us bread and bacon.

Still, the behavior of the Germans remained dangerously inconsistent. One night, as some of them left the house, they tarried long enough to burn down the stables where twelve of our girls were hiding. Luckily, these refugees managed to escape in time, but we never learned what happened to them after that.

As the Russian forces advanced, fires in the area became more frequent. At night, the flames ignited the sky with an eerie, menacing light. And then the entire house began to rumble and shake with the tremors of war. Those of us who had been through it before reacted more casually than the Polish woman and her three daughters, who sank to their knees and begged God to spare them. At one point, they decided to seek refuge in the forest, insisting that we come along.

"You have been through so much! It would be

criminal if you lost your lives now!"

I agreed that it would be sad indeed, but could not bring myself to leave this warm, comfortable haven. "We will be all right," I assured them. As they fled into the woods, Magda and I stayed behind, accepting the reverberations of the bombs and artillery fire as a matter of course. By now, it seemed hard to imagine a lifestyle that did not have constant gunfire and human destruction as a backdrop. Would we ever again be able to live as normal human beings, performing daily chores and conversing about matters not associated with immediate survival?

Could life ever become ordinary and predictable again, with some sort of pattern or reason attached to it?

What would it feel like not to be desperate?

After three days of constant siege, the area suddenly became still. It was such an ominous silence that we dared not trust it, but the traffic on the streets had vanished as well, and that was certainly an indication of something.

As I looked out the window, I saw a Russian soldier passing on horseback. His tall, fur Cossack hat made his nationality easily discernible and, casting caution to the winds, I ran from the house, waving a white towel to attract his attention. He stopped and waited for me to approach, then asked if any of the German Gestapo were about. I told him no, and he promptly asked if we had any vodka in the house. Once again, I told him no, and then explained where we were from, and the way we had come here.

"You have nothing to fear," he said. "You have been liberated."

Magda had come up behind me as we spoke, and now she and I fairly pulled him from his horse to hug and kiss him for bringing us such good news. As we jumped about, singing and dancing for joy, he momentarily observed our antics with obvious amusement and then remounted his horse and slowly rode away.

"Do you think it's true, Mama?" Magda asked excitedly. "We've heard such rumors before. Perhaps we shouldn't presume too much."

"But there is a difference this time. Listen how quiet it's become! And the streets are totally deserted. It can only mean the end of the war. It's happening, my girl! This nightmare is finally coming to an end!"

We raced back to the house and saw that the Polish woman and her daughters had returned from hiding. They had been making a regular practice of running into the woods each night and returning in the morning. When we told them what the Russian soldier had said, they remained somewhat skeptical, but on the whole seemed highly pleased.

"If it is truly over, then it is because of you that we have been spared," the Polish woman insisted quickly. She seemed to feel that God had spared the house because of us. She was a very religious woman and believed He had performed a miracle in our honor.

It was a time when such things are easily accepted; anything and everything seemed possible now. The miracle itself could not be denied, because everything around us had been totally destroyed. Only this farmhouse remained untouched.

Later in the day, as the Russian troops began to roll through the town in their huge tanks, we met them in the streets and offered hot coffee, which they gratefully accepted. The parade of soldiers, tanks and arms continued throughout the day. It gave us a blissfully secure feeling to look out the window and see them there. I remembered a morning, so long ago, when I had looked out another window to see the Jewish people of our village being herded through the streets. That had been the start of the nightmare, and apparently this was the end of it.

"I think we should leave now," I told Magda. "This is still a battlefield, and if somehow the Germans manage to push back the Russians, even for a little while, we would be in danger here."

As Magda hesitated, I knew she was considering the immediate advantages in remaining where we were. During the time we had remained alone in the house, we had been given a generous supply of potatoes and cabbages to cook for ourselves. Our basic needs had been well attended to, and life back out on the road could not hope to compare to this.

"We have no choice," I told her quietly. It is time for us to leave. You do understand, don't you?"

"Y-Yes, I know. I was only thinking that it would be nice if things could always be the way they are now."

"Someday soon they will be even better," I promised her. "Come along, my child."

What sense of security we had enjoyed while living at the farmhouse was quickly shattered when we returned to the streets. Once again, we began to doubt the war had really ended, that we would be permitted to move about freely, and that we would actually manage to survive and return home.

I kept these doubts to myself, but had only to look at Magda to see she felt the same. All in a moment, the tension had returned to her face, and she glanced and moved about as furtively as before. I knew then that we would continue to be plagued by the Gestapo. In our imaginings and in our dreams, their heavy footsteps and threatening voices would resound for years to come.

A new snowfall had made walking even more difficult than before, and our wooden-soled shoes caused us to slide about precariously. Like drunken sailors, we lurched from one side of the road to the other, encountering along the way huge numbers of Russian troops, who impeded our progress even more. Now and again, we would be stopped and asked to identify ourselves, but no one bothered us, and in one instance, a Russian soldier even offered us some bread and marmalade.

"Do not be afraid," we were constantly told. "The Gestapo will not bother you any more."

To receive such constant reassurances was in itself indicative of the way we appeared to others. All the fear and uncertainty had come back to roost inside us, churning about like a familiar old friend. I found myself taking deep, gasping breaths, an anxious habit I had fallen into when we first arrived at Auschwitz.

"Are you all right, Mama?" Magda asked at one point, and I hastily assured her I was.

"It is only that this walking has become so strenuous. In those few days at the farmhouse, I seem to have become a little soft. It doesn't take long to lose one's endurance. But I will get it back again."

I could see she did not totally believe me and developed the practice of watching me very closely after that.

So many times throughout our incarceration, we had reversed the mother-daughter roles, depending upon who had the greatest amount of strength at the time, and who was most in need. In other circumstances, I might have found this a very interesting subject to contemplate, but as it was, I could only resent the fact that this girl had been cheated of her childhood, and now could never again reclaim it.

As if to underscore this thought, that evening we arrived in a small village which was literally blanketed with dead German soldiers. They lay all over the roads, their bodies frozen hard amid ice-crusted pools of blood, a ghastly sight that would remain with us for a long time to come. Still, we had learned to lock a certain part of ourselves away from the horror, and this impervious part made a hasty calculation of the fact that the boots of these dead soldiers were quite new, while our own shoes were in shreds and falling from our feet.

We looked about for boots in the smallest sizes we could find and proceeded to pull them off the bodies of their dead owners. This was accomplished with some difficulty, but when we at last had their shoes on our own feet, we found that walking became much easier.

The militia found a place for us to stay that night and the next day we continued on our journey.

Traveling with no real sense of direction through high snowdrifts is somewhat like walking on another planet. Everything looked so much the same, we could easily have been going in circles. The terrain stretched out endlessly, with no great change in appearance even after miles of walking. At one point, we entered a thick forest, and it was not until I was certain we had lost our way that we finally found a path that led us out of it.

When we reached a well-traveled highway, in

all directions we saw overturned automobiles, wagons, bicycles and dead frozen bodies lying in beds of personal belongings that included housewares and linens.

"Instead of pillowcases, I wish they had brought along some food," Magda said despondently.

We sifted through everything, but there was nothing edible. Our only hope was to reach the city of Bromberg, where we would be able to find sufficient food—and transportation to get us home. At this moment, however, I could no longer assume we were even headed toward Bromberg.

"What should we do?" Magda asked. "There is nothing behind us, and there doesn't appear to be anything ahead of us, either."

"Well, we know what's behind us, but we can't be sure what's ahead. Let's keep going," I told her.

Some time later, my instincts proved correct, for we finally came upon Bromberg, although it was not the city we remembered. It had been heavily bombarded and lay in ruins, with fires still burning here and there. We saw no sign of local residents, only the military police patrolling the streets. As we stood looking about, one of them approached us and asked if we needed a place to stay.

"Yes, and some food, if that's possible," I said. "We haven't had anything to eat in a very long time."

"Well, come along then," the officer said. After walking some distance, we arrived at the home of a high-ranking German officer, an exceptionally beautiful place in the midst of so much devastation. At one time, the German officer had been living in a four-room apartment upstairs, and his housekeeper was still living downstairs.

When she opened the door and saw us standing there in the company of the Russian patrol, she became as uncooperative as her situation would permit.

"These ladies need a place to stay," the officer explained quickly, but the woman shook her head, insisting that there wasn't any way to accommodate us.

"Then you will think of a way," the Russian told her flatly, and prodding us forward, encouraged us to enter the house.

"They will have to stay in the basement. There is no other place for them," the housekeeper snapped disdainfully.

"They will stay in the apartment upstairs," the officer retorted angrily, and knocked her to the side with a swift, hard slap to the face.

"I can't allow this!" the woman protested hysterically, but as the Russian advanced upon her, she quickly handed him the key.

"Go on up," he told us. "If this wretched hag creates any further problems, I can assure you she will live to regret it."

The woman cowered in a corner of the hall, glowering at us hatefully as we climbed the staircase and entered a truly heavenly place.

Perhaps our imaginations have embellished it

somewhat, but I remember the furnishings to be exquisite, with soft, luxurious bedding and—oh, wonder of wonders—a large, gleaming bathtub.

Meanwhile, Magda had discovered a pantry filled with food. After we had sampled much of what we found there, we decided to have a bath. Since the water pipes leading to the house had been damaged, there was no water unless one of us went out and brought some in from a community well or carried in some fresh snow. For this first warm bath, we melted some snow in a large pot on the stove.

Later, we sat down at a long mahogany table and ate a truly delicious meal. The pantry had been amply stocked with a variety of preserves and other succulent foods that we attacked with great gusto.

Once we'd had our fill, we fell across the large bed and tested it for comfort.

"Not as firm as the boards in the barracks," Magda said in mock criticism. "I fear this ridiculously soft mattress may give us curvature of the spine."

"Good!" I said with a languid sigh. "I've always wanted curvature of the spine."

"And all that food will make you fat and matronly," Magda warned.

"Perfect!" I said. "What is more attractive than a fat, matronly woman with curvature of the spine?"

" . . . wearing army boots!" Magda retorted at once, and as we conjured up this sight, we were overcome by such a fit of uncontrollable laughter that the housekeeper downstairs must have thought we had taken leave of our senses. As we lay there, we continued to embellish the appearance of this imaginary woman until we could both see her quite clearly, walking casually through the streets of our town, conducting her affairs in a nice dress, but with a bald, shining head that had been topped with a rather odd contraption of a hat.

Our lighthearted mood had suddenly caused us to recall a very real incident in the barracks involving a number of our girls.

While the Germans had liberally laced our food with something intended to stop the monthly onset of menstruation, many of the girls had continued to menstruate anyway, which necessitated the use of certain sanitary supplies. These were coarse, pleated pads which, in cold weather, the girls would sometimes unfold and wear on their heads as a protective covering.

For the first time, we could see how totally ludicrous this was, and once again, were overpowered by gales of laughter, until finally the last of our anxieties and tensions eased away. Then we quickly fell into a deep, exhausted sleep in that beautiful bed as soft as a cloud and did not stir until morning.

We remained in that house for approximately two weeks, and would experience many good and bad things along the way.

The German housekeeper, although obviously intimidated by the Russian patrol officer's threats, became no friendlier in the days that followed our arrival. We sensed her presence in every corner of the house, although she made a deliberate effort to avoid us.

Our circumstances, however, necessitated a certain amount of travel up and down the stairs, especially because of the need to bring in water. Had we been able to bring ourselves to forgo the pleasure of a cleansing bath, the trips to the well might have been made less frequently, but we could not bring ourselves to give up this newfound luxury. We would go to this common meeting place in the center of town, where the crowds in no way prevented us from getting the water we needed.

On one such outing, we happened upon the same Russian patrol officer who had helped us gain entrance into the house we were now living in. He inquired about our comfort and the general disposition of the German housekeeper.

"She is not happy having us under her roof," Magda admitted, "but does not voice her displeasure. If anything, she makes a great point of avoiding us."

"If she ever opens her mouth, you need only report her to the nearest patrol officer. They will take care of her. For that matter, I would take great pleasure in tending to her myself."

"We don't want any trouble," I told him then. "We are grateful for the use of that lovely place. It is enough to be able to come in out of the cold and have decent food to eat."

"You need decent clothes as well," the Russian retorted bluntly. "Take whatever you find in the closets and drawers. You are entitled to them now."

Magda and I looked at one another with amazement. We had grown so accustomed to having others pilfer and steal from us that we had never considered the possibility that this situation might one day be reversed. And yet here we were being told to loot this private home and take whatever we wanted for our own use or to barter.

"Don't stand there looking like fools!" the Russian snorted. "There is no morality in war. You may be sure that the Germans have stripped your own home of everything you hold dear. Once you are ready to admit that to yourselves, you won't have any second thoughts about taking whatever is available to you."

It had not occurred to me, until that moment, that I had held a picture in my mind of our house as it once was, with everything intact and with its warm, secure atmosphere undisturbed. More than likely, the house would not even be standing, but if it were, I knew it was absurd to think that it might still resemble anything we had called home.

As we walked back to the apartment, I told

Magda we would look about and see what we could find. We needed things to wear and things to sell to assure a safe journey home. Having been officially given permission to loot as much as we wished, it seemed best to take advantage of this opportunity.

In examining the personal affects in the apartment, we concluded that the German officer had not been married, because there was no evidence of women's clothing or jewelry. But there was a fine collection of men's wear, shirts and trousers made of warm, sturdy fabrics which would withstand the rigors of our journey much better than the rags we were wearing.

Once we'd begun, the scavenging process became easier. We searched every nook and cranny, gathering a good supply of wristwatches, rings, gems and other negotiable items. Then, clothed in our new masculine attire, we paraded before the mirror and tried to make light of the fact that we were quite the strangest-looking pair one could ever hope to meet.

We would not soon forget the shock of seeing ourselves for the first time, since these hideous reflections made it difficult to believe that we would ever again look totally human. It helped to be clean again, but it was impossible to erase the black circles under our eyes, the hunted looks and the sharp-boned features. We were vain enough to be repulsed by what we saw, fearing that some permanent damage had been done that would make it necessary to retreat into dark shadows for the rest of our lives. Back home, I could not imagine walking through the streets in daylight looking as I did. I had grown so used to seeing others who looked the same that I had very nearly forgotten there were people in this world who looked normal, attractive, even beautiful. How we would suffer by comparison, appearing monstrous and grotesque, while others pitied us but found they could no longer accept us.

I did not speak of these things to Magda, although she must have known a similar or even greater anguish at the loss of her robust good looks. The vanity of youth does not deal well with such things. I remembered how she had once worried about a freckle, or a wisp of hair that refused to lie properly. She had felt such things to be catastrophic, as young girls do, and now must have felt that her entire life was over. Still, we kept up the charade of laughing at ourselves, for it seemed the only thing to do.

After a few days of wearing men's clothes along with the army boots we had stolen from the dead German soldiers, we gave no further thought to our unusual appearance. We therefore lost our ability to anticipate the reactions of others, most specifically, the reaction of the German housekeeper who got a glimpse of us one day as we left the house to go to the well.

"Stop! Stop!" she cried out suddenly and, as we looked about, she flew at us like a predatory bird, clawing at our faces and spewing forth a shower of guttural German that was easily translated just by its sound. What little I was able to interpret accurately had something to do with desecrating the memory of the German officer who had worn these clothes. She extolled him as a kind, gentle man who had regarded her throughout her years of service more as a friend than a servant.

"You are not fit to touch his garments with your vile hands!" she shrieked. "How dare you presume to act with such familiarity! Nothing personal is to be removed from his apartment. Herr Engel was the product of princely blood. As long as I am here, I will see to it that the sanctity of his home is preserved as he would have wished." As she ranted on, she worked frantically at the buttons of our shirts, trying to unfasten them so that she might strip these garments from our backs.

At first, I hardly knew what to make of her, but in time, her chronic whining became tiresome, and at last I was overcome by a wave of violent anger. Grabbing her by the hair, I flung her away from me like a sack of laundry. As she slid across the highly polished wood floor, I fought the urge to pounce upon her and beat her senseless.

"I do not want your blood on my hands so I will let you go on living!" I spat out hatefully. "Still, if you make one more threatening move toward my girl or me, I will see to it that the Russian patrol officer finishes you off. He has already volunteered to do the job any time we may choose to request it. Your home is no more sacred than that of any other human being on this earth. Because of this abysmal war, we Jews have endured the loss of our homes, our loved ones and everything that humans hold dear. What few inconveniences you have suffered are nothing compared to what we have seen and experienced at the hands of the Germans. If I could have one wish, I would wish that you might know a hundred years of that kind of torture! What a pitiful, selfish creature you are to be able to sit in the midst of all this devastation and concern yourself with the disposition of a few pieces of clothing. You, with that blind allegiance and exaggerated sense of your own importance are the sort who make an Adolph Hitler possible! He preyed upon your desire to believe you were superior to any other race of people on earth when, in fact, you are less than the human dung I once had to collect from the latrines to use as fertilizer on the gardens of our camp. Those latrines and your head are filled with the same manure. Now, sit where you are and be still, or I will personally see to it that this is your last day on earth!"

With that, I grabbed Magda by the arm and yanked her out of the house, moving with urgent haste away from that woman and her malicious bigotry.

When I next looked at her, I saw that Magda was laughing and asked what she found so amusing.

"That housekeeper!" Magda chuckled. "I've

never seen anyone so terrified. She looked as if she were going to wet her pants!"

"If she does, we'll give her a pair of Herr Engel's to wear," I snapped, still angry but beginning to see the humor in the situation. "Don't get me started on that wretched woman again. She is beyond contempt!"

Later in the day, when we returned to the house, the housekeeper was nowhere in sight, and we went back up to our rooms without further incident. The place was so quiet for the balance of the day that a soft knock at our door shortly after dark caused us to leap from our chairs as if someone had sounded a trumpet.

As I opened the door a crack, I heard the housekeeper say, *"Bitte...."* asking me to please open the door a bit farther.

I did as she asked and then saw that she had a large covered tray in her hands. She quickly explained she had just finished her cooking for the week and thought we might like a more substantial meal than we had been able to prepare for ourselves from the pantry stock.

"There is no reason why we cannot get along," she added. "At least it is best if we try."

Since she had made no move to enter the apartment without my permission, I allowed her to enter and watched as she placed the tray on a large oak table by the window.

"Everything is scarce, but I have been able to fashion a kind of German stew which you might care for. It has good, thick gravy at least. If you like it, there is more," she assured us.

As she moved to leave, I hastily thanked her, and then looked at Magda as if wonders would never cease.

After we were alone, we examined the tray and saw it had been tastefully arranged. The woman was obviously accustomed to working for the well-to-do and knew how to cater to their needs with efficiency and elegance.

"Can you imagine it?" I marveled. "After all the horrible things I said to her, she brings us all this!"

"You were totally justified in what you said," Magda insisted. "Perhaps she realizes it now."

As we took our places at opposite ends of the table, Magda poured the hot tea she had prepared earlier, and we proceeded to sample the rich, brown stew that filled the room with its fragrant, spicy aroma.

Suddenly, Magda leaped from her chair and jerked the spoon from my hand. "No!" she cried. "Don't eat any of it! She may be trying to poison us!"

It was a possibility I hadn't stopped to consider, but now that I had, my first thought was that we were both suffering the effects of an overworked imagination.

"The housekeeper has not been kind, and has made no secret of her animosity toward us," I admitted. "But poisoning is quite another matter. It might well be that we are beginning to suffer the delusions of paranoia."

"Still, poisoning the food would be the easiest way to get rid of us," Magda reasoned. "She could always claim afterward that we died of the effects of the concentration camp. And we would certainly be in no position to refute her claims."

As she spoke, I stared longingly at the thick, brown stew, thinking how like Hungarian goulash it was. I had grown a bit tired of the bread and jams in the pantry, which were more of a snack than a meal. Here at last was a hearty supper that would stick to our ribs and help us regain our strength—unless, of course, Magda was right. I knew it was not a risk worth taking, and so, along with Magda's encouragement, went out late that night and buried the stew in the snow.

Life in the apartment was awkward after that. We read things into everything the housekeeper said and did. It seemed to us she watched us more closely, perhaps in an attempt to detect some affects of the poison. She encouraged us to spend more time downstairs, and to share her meals with her. We always declined, hoping our distrust of her would be mistaken for shyness.

And then one day our residency in the apartment came to an abrupt end. The police informed us that they needed the space for their own officers and soldiers, and we would have to vacate the premises. We took this news in stride—it was typical of what we had come to expect.

The miracle was that we had been allowed to remain there for fourteen days, the longest we had been allowed to remain anywhere.

The day we left, the housekeeper stood silently by, her face stiff and expressionless, as if she did not wish to betray her true feelings.

"She was glad to see us go," Magda said, once we had left the place. "She was trying hard not to smile. I was right about her. And now I am *sure* the food was poisoned!"

As we stepped outside, a key slowly turned. A cautious hand had locked the door behind us, seeming to substantiate Magda's suspicions.

Once again, our faces became rigid with fear. It was not yet over. Perhaps it never would be.

I tried to envision the housekeeper's reaction when she went upstairs to examine the apartment. We had been meticulous in our habits, but could not resist taking the photo of Adolph Hitler from the wall and smashing it against a chair. The pieces had been gathered and neatly wrapped in a towel, but she could not fail to find them. It had been a small act of revenge, but totally satisfying.

Now, back on the streets, we ambled aimlessly. Without any concrete plan, it seemed important merely to keep moving.

"What should we do now, Mama? Where should we go?" Magda asked, in a small, apprehensive voice.

"Well, we will have to find another place to stay,

of course, if only for the night. Our luck has been pretty good so far. Perhaps it will continue."

But we were destined to sleep in a hayloft that night, as it was the only structure close at hand when at last an overpowering fatigue possessed us. We had hoped to travel farther that day, but the weeks in the apartment had weakened our resistance and, by dusk, we were forced to stop.

Still, it was not the worst place in the world for the loft was filled with hay and, after we had eaten a portion of the meager ration we had brought along, we began to shift the warm, soft straw around to fashion our bed for the night.

We tried to concoct some kind of plan for the following day, but quickly fell into a deep, exhausted sleep which would have lasted until morning had it not been for a sudden, unexpected visit.

As we slept, a small, stray party of German officers came into the barn beneath us, and we awoke to hear them moving about in a manner that told us they were settling in for the night.

Their conversation drifted up to us through the wide cracks in the floor, and their general mood was cause for much apprehension. They were avid in their opinions and also extremely vocal. In loud, boisterous tones, they blamed the Jews for everything that was wrong with the world and, more significantly, the fall of Germany.

"Hitler had the answer!" one of them insisted loudly, pounding his fist sharply against a wooden beam that made the floor of the loft tremble. "If the world had only been smart enough to listen!"

"Well, they will learn," another said, somewhat threateningly. "Those Jews are the scourge of the earth. There is never anything but misery connected with that filthy breed. They pass it on wherever they go. Things would have turned out differently if our Fuehrer had received adequate support. But I will continue to remain in his service whenever I see a Jew. Just let one of them show themselves, and I will be pleased to do my duty as a German soldier."

Magda and I exchanged horrified glances at this, realizing now that we could not afford to be discovered.

"Be still," I told her, merely mouthing the words. "Do not move."

She nodded silently and, for the next hour or so, we hardly dared breathe as the volatile conversation beneath us continued.

"I am starving," one of the soldiers announced suddenly. "There must be something on this farm that is decent enough to eat."

"I've already examined the main house," another of the officers said. But perhaps there are still a few farm animals about. Let's go and see."

As quickly as they left the barn, Magda turned to me and said, "This is our chance. Let's make a run for it."

"No!" I told her. "There is no way that we could escape detection. There isn't even a tree anywhere to hide behind. They would be sure to see us."

As we continued to debate the pros and cons of leaving the loft, a raucous volley of sound assailed our ears and, amid great screeching and squawking, the officers returned to the barn, their arms filled with frightened chickens. Through the widest crack in the floor, we could see they were attempting to twist the necks of these birds so that they could roast them for dinner. The chickens, of course, had other ideas and flew about in a hysterical frenzy, beating their wings so desperately that many managed to escape. As we watched in horror, a number of them flew up into the loft, passing over our heads with wild cries and a thick flurry of feathers. As they flew by, their talons raked through our hair and, as we tried to beat them off, they became all the more animated. Not daring to cry out, we worked with feverish haste, trying to extricate ourselves from the clutches of these wild, crazy birds so we could direct them back outside. But while we were determined to get them out of the loft, they seemed no less determined to fly back in. It was a truly horrendous experience, what with the German soldiers directly beneath us. We were certain that the pandemonium would eventually lead them to investigate the loft. After everything we had already survived, it seemed we were now fated to be undone by a flock of hysterical chickens.

As we stubbornly continued to push the birds

through the window of the loft, they retaliated by shredding our skin with their long, sharp claws. The pain was excruciating, and all the moreso because we dared not utter a sound. Our eyes were blurred with tears, and we had to bite down hard to keep from crying out.

Meanwhile, the officers had already slaughtered some of the chickens. Suddenly, one of the birds, decapitated by a small ax that one of the Germans had found, began flying about the barn, showering blood in every direction. It was the most gruesome thing that had happened thus far, but it provided the diversion needed to keep us from being discovered. As the officers pursued the headless chicken with loud shouts and laughter, our own movements upstairs were effectively overshadowed. By the time the bird had bled to death, we'd managed to clear the loft of all the other chickens and were settled back down in the hay, as motionless as statues.

We managed a few hours sleep that night and, the next morning, when we awoke, the soldiers had already gone. In our own best interests, we decided to remain in the loft for a while and give them a good head start.

Encountering these soldiers had been an unfortunate but valuable experience. We had wanted to believe there was no further need to fear the Germans, but now realized this was a careless attitude, at least partially provoked by the arrival of the Russians. We could not again afford to be lulled into a false sense of security. There were still a number of fanatical Germans about, angry, embittered people who could not accept the loss of the war and the fall of Adolph Hitler.

As we nibbled at a small sliver of bread and cheese, we watched the sun rise in the sky, and tried to guess the time by its gradually changing position.

"I think it will be safe to go now," I said at last, though we glanced about with apprehensive curiosity as we descended from the loft into the barn.

Quite obviously, the Germans had slain many more chickens than they needed, because a number of dead carcasses were strewn about, their twisted necks attesting to the rage and violence in these men.

"What a waste," Magda sighed. "What a pointless slaughter."

"Better the birds than us," I told her. "You can see now what would have happened to us at their hands."

"I am so tired of being hated," Magda said. "I don't understand any of this. I never shall!"

"You and a few million others," I retorted bitterly. "Come along, my girl. We must find our way back to the company of other people—other refugees and Russian soldiers. It was foolish to stray so far away from them. It could easily have cost us our lives."

And so, another day of seemingly endless walking was under way. We chose our directions instinctively, following first one path and then another, until at last we arrived at a large, rambling house that was obviously inhabited, since it literally reverberated with sound.

Our knock on the door was quickly answered by a young girl I recognized from our group. She welcomed us with open arms, although the house was so packed with people, I could not imagine where we would stay.

"There are about eighty of us here," the girl advised. "It will be extremely crowded, but we will manage."

Perhaps it was our very numbers that forced us into organizing our efforts, a system that worked out extremely well in the days ahead. In small, determined teams, we blanketed the area in search of food and clothing. Our plundering was not immediately curtailed; if anything, it was readily encouraged by several Russian soldiers who, as it turned out, were of Jewish extraction.

At the end of each day, we would return to the house and share our bounty. We no longer had any qualms about collecting whatever was at hand, because we had long since decided that the Russian soldier had been right. He had said that our homes were being plundered, too, so all was fair in love and war. It now seemed a most equitable arrangement, and I could not imagine why I had ever been concerned about it.

While we stayed in that house, slowly, steadily,

some trace of color returned to Magda's face—a quiet, subtle miracle like a tiny rose in bloom. At first I thought I only imagined the improvement in her looks but soon it was altogether obvious, even to her. There came a day when I saw her pause in front of a hall mirror, pushing her short, wispy hair first one way and then another, for the first time exhibiting some trace of womanly interest in her appearance and what might be done about it. I could see she felt hopeful now, that she was actually considering the possibility of one day looking attractive again, not just passably human, but even attractive. In that moment, I felt an incredible joy for her, knowing she had recaptured an aspect of youth to which she was so richly entitled. Walking up behind her, I told her what a difference some decent clothes, a good diet and the safety and security of home would make.

"You look so much better already!" I assured her. "Before long, you will be the prettiest girl in town, with dozens of admirers, and a wonderful, exciting future before you."

"That sort of life seems so long ago and far away," Magda said thoughtfully. "Pretty dresses ... parties ... and worrying about whether or not your hair ribbons match your eyes. It is difficult to even admit to such vanity now. I am sure I could never totally immerse myself in it again. I would not even want to."

"Still, you have earned your share of happy,

carefree times, and I shall see you have them," I said. "You cannot help the bitterness you feel, Magda, but it would be a mistake to let it twist your entire life. If you do that, you will be perpetuating this war for all time. Let it die in your mind as it is dying on the battlefields. Try to remember that everything is not ugliness and devastation, although that is all you have seen for a very long time. In other parts of the world, there is beauty and joy, and you can be a part of that again."

"You needn't worry," Magda replied, and gave me just the hint of a confident smile. "We will come through this, Mama. And we will have a good life. You will see."

It seemed that every optimistic outlook had to be tested, for no sooner had we adopted this attitude than an order was issued that prevented all further looting. This put an abrupt end to our food supply and, although our health had greatly improved, we still had a long way to go and dared not lose ground.

We hadn't any idea where the next town might be, or how we could hope to get there, because all means of transportation had been bombed out by the ongoing fighting.

And now, in our questionable state of liberation, we found that the Polish people were becoming extremely anti-Semitic, making no secret of their feelings once they learned we were Jewish.

In addition, we heard that during the evacuation fifteen of our girls had been shot down, twelve had died when the Gestapo burned down the house they were living in, and ten others had been hospitalized in very serious condition. Although we were no longer incarcerated, the war and the hate continued as the Russians and Germans fought fiercely around us.

Moving through the streets in a state of total confusion, I tried to think of where to turn and what to do next. I was so deep in thought that I barely heard a soft, muffled sound somewhere behind me. When at last it registered in my mind, I turned to see two young girls who had been so wounded by shrapnel fragments they were unable to walk.

As their eyes pleaded with me for assistance, I helped them onto an abandoned sled and pulled them to a hospital a number of miles away. It was a slow, agonizing journey, and the girls would cry out in pain whenever the runners of the sled struck an obstruction in the road. The trip was no more pleasant for me, since their combined weight was more than I had anticipated and the road was not level, necessitating a hard, uphill climb in certain spots, with rocks and potholes everywhere. When at last I saw the hospital up ahead, I thought it must be a mirage. But as we neared, it proved real enough. Although it was extremely crowded, I was able to get the girls admitted. They clung to my hands when I moved to leave, refusing to release me until I had promised to come back and visit them.

"We cannot thank you enough," they murmured over and over again. "We must see you again."

"Yes, yes," I hastily agreed. "But I must be leaving now. I have left my daughter behind, and she will begin to worry. Later, when I come back, I will bring her with me. You shall have the opportunity to meet one another."

They smiled happily at that, and I knew I would have no choice except to honor this promise. They would be waiting every moment until we returned.

Of course, the second visit was extremely difficult, because we all knew it was the last.

"What will happen to us without you?" the girls cried out despondently. Although I had no real answer, I tried to remain cheerful and encouraging, citing instances in which civilians and Russian soldiers had helped us. "You will find people more accommodating than you would expect," I told them, carefully avoiding mention of those who had tried their best to do us in.

Soon afterward, we learned that some military trains were still in service and, after making our way to the railroad station, we sat for hours, waiting for just such a train to arrive. At long last, some cars came rattling down the tracks and stopped at the platform. We glanced about hurriedly to see if anyone was watching and, when we felt certain our actions would not be noticed, we climbed into one of the empty wagons and waited for the train to move again. As soon as we felt the first suggestion of motion, we settled back for the ride, totally unaware of where we might be heading. It felt so good to be riding instead of walking that, for the moment, it was enough just to be going somewhere.

We traveled this way for several days. The weather was bitterly cold, and we had to huddle together for warmth. Occasionally, the train would stop while the soldiers went to neighboring farms and slaughtered a few chickens and ducks for their own meals.

On the third day, we learned we were heading toward Krakow, which seemed altogether miraculous, since I knew we had to go through Krakow to reach Czechoslovakia.

"At least we're traveling in the right direction," I said with a deep sigh. On more than one occasion I had worried that we might actually be getting farther and farther from home.

The journey to Krakow took eight days, but finally we arrived to discover that this city showed no evidence of the war. Moving slowly through the marketplace, we took notice of the normal activities in which these people were engaged, feeling as if we were moving through a dream. This was not reality as we knew it.

We sold some of the clothing and jewelry we had carried in our backpacks, and with the money we bought food. After we had eaten a portion of it, I asked a gentleman in the streets if there were any Jews from the concentration camps anywhere about.

"There is a building up ahead, the American Joint Committee, as it is known. It was specifically set up for those who are returning. Food and shelter are available there."

Following the man's instructions, we soon arrived there and were immediately asked to register. We were asked our names, point of origin and which concentration camp we had come from. Then we received 100 zlotys, some food, and shelter in the form of a large room with straw pallets on the floor to sleep on. A week after we arrived, this place was already crowded to capacity.

The food was extremely poor, though, and many chose to go out into the streets and beg. Magda and I continued to dispose of the various items in our knapsack to get something decent to eat, and on one occasion, even patronized a local restaurant. It was an extraordinary experience. Suddenly we became conscious of the need for proper table manners and a type of social behavior we had long since abandoned. Even with the added convenience of silverware, there was still a certain compulsion to pick up the food with our hands and hastily shove it into our mouths before anyone could take it away from us.

Although everyone in the place was preoccupied with their own affairs, I could not help but feel we were the center of attention, that everyone was staring at us because of our strange garb and clumsy behavior. I had not felt nearly so conspicuous in war-torn villages and towns, but here, where everything remained so graciously civilized, I began to feel like an alien on my own planet.

The restaurant experience was not as pleasant as I had hoped and, as we returned to the community center, I began to feel more at ease, perhaps in the same way a stray heifer feels when it knows it is on its way back to the herd. Having for such a long time been treated and thought of as cattle, it was not difficult to identify with these poor, dumb creatures, and to feel out of place unless we were with a motley crew who looked and acted as we did. A sort of herd instinct had replaced all prior feelings of confidence and human dignity, another way of saying that the camp had not only stripped us of everything material, but many intangible things as well.

With a sudden impatience borne of the desire to regain my own identity, I expressed my desire to leave the center, though I was warned against it. The organization advised that it was quite dangerous to travel without some form of identification and, since I could not argue with the logic in this, we made the necessary applications, and soon several more weeks had passed.

At that point, I made the decision to go on without the necessary papers. Living on the community center floor had become intolerable. The place was infested with lice and, while we had been able to avoid them in many of the other unsanitary places we had stayed, we now contracted them along with everyone else and suffered as they did, because there was no way to disinfect ourselves.

Early one morning, we went out to the market, bought bread, butter, honey and salami and packed up to leave. At the time of our departure, we were a party of six, including a seventeen-year-old girl who remained glued to my side as if her very life depended on it. She spoke only Hungarian, whereas I knew enough Russian, Polish and Bohemian to obtain directions and whatever other information was necessary to us.

We walked to the railroad station where a freight train was being loaded with coal. Without hesitation, we climbed on top of the coal in the back of the train and waited for it to depart. The train did not move until the following morning, and then journeyed on for four days and four nights. We endured the elements with only a few military blankets for cover.

When at last we arrived in Kraszna, our trip abruptly ended when the train was bombed out and we were forced to flee for our lives.

Unlike Krakow, Kraszna was a dreadful sight to behold. It had been totally destroyed, and the streets were deserted, except for an occasional person wandering about aimlessly. We had fallen back into the death and destruction to which we were accustomed. We reacted as we had in the past, walking along stealthily and holding on to one another for reassurance.

"How can we get to Slovakia?" I asked the next person we passed, observing the pained cynicism in his eyes as he replied.

"How do you get there? You walk." Pointing out a direction, he added, "Go that way. Walk to Yaslo and once you are there, it may be possible to get a train."

We did as we were told, walking through the deep snow in that February of 1945, until at last we arrived in a small village and encountered a Jewish family who had been in hiding for more than a year. They were staying in the attic of a home that belonged to some Polish people, hidden away with an inadequate amount of air and food. Still, these compassionate Jews took us in with them for a day and night, and shared what little they had. I noticed that the eldest among them had trouble standing; she was so weak and frail that the wind could have blown her away. I had an ominous feeling about her and am inclined to doubt she ever saw her homeland again.

After we left that family, we continued our march through first one village and then another. Having lost all track of time, we began to lose touch with reality. With blistered feet and heavy hearts, we trudged on, employing a slow, mechanical pace that proved the least exhausting. All things had become secondary to putting one foot in front of the other with a kind of relentless precision that automatically carried us forward. What we viewed along the way had ceased to disturb us. Everything was murky and bleak, a fitting backdrop for our general mood.

After several days of walking, we reached yet another small village close to the Slovak border. There we paused for a night's rest and the next morning, I accelerated my efforts to find a way to Slovakia, which was known as Slovensko in Czechoslovakia.

"You will have to go through a forest," one of the villagers informed me. "It is a dangerous journey, as there are land mines everywhere."

Here was a complication I had not previously considered, but once I did, I knew we were no match for it.

As if reading my thoughts, the villager said, "If you are determined to make your way along this route, you will need a capable guide."

"You mean there *is* such a person?" I asked, as if wonders would never cease.

"Yes, there is one among us who knows his way around the mines. For a price, he will walk along with you and show you the way."

Once I had obtained this gentleman's name, I went to see him and explained our situation. "I haven't any money, but I can give you two very nice shirts for your trouble."

When he agreed to accompany us, I thanked him profusely, refusing to consider any of the risks involved. If he was not as skilled at mine detection as he professed to be, we would all pay a bitter price for it.

When I told the others what arrangements I had made, they reacted with guarded enthusiasm.

"I know what you are thinking," I told them, "and I would suggest you think about something else."

Despite our apprehensions, we all began to laugh, which helped release some of the tension.

The following day, we became increasingly apprehensive of our plan to travel through a forest of land mines, for our guide was extremely pessimistic, or so it seemed. He did his best to dissuade us, repeatedly emphasizing the very great dangers involved. He was a stern-faced Pole whose attitude alone was enough to discourage anyone. It was, of course, difficult for us to justify our need to take this risk, but we had become obsessed with the thought of returning home, if only to see who else had survived. Since these were not his people, he could not have understood the importance of the journey.

"But you told me that you knew the path," I reminded him. "And several other villagers have assured me of the same thing. They tell me you frequently walk through this forest."

"Only because it is difficult to avoid, if one hopes to get from here to there. I have made a point of uncovering the safest path, but now, everything is covered with snow, making it easy to lose one's bearings. I will do the best I can, but you must understand that I cannot guarantee your safety."

"No one has guaranteed our safety in a very long time," I said, a trifle irritably. "If you will take your chances, we will take ours."

"I don't mean to offend you," he said then. "I am much more sympathetic to your cause than you might imagine. Let me remind you that it is not common for someone to enter into a life-threatening situation for the price of two shirts. Obviously, that could not have been my only motive."

"Yes, yes, I understand that. You must forgive me. Please don't mistake my impatience for rudeness. It is just that we are extremely anxious to return home. It had not occurred to us until recently that other members of our family might have survived. But now that *we* have survived, we have begun to consider this possibility, and it is something we simply must know!"

"Very well then," the Pole said. "We will walk through the forest—in tight, single file. You must not stray from the line even a fraction of an inch. You will follow in my footsteps, placing your feet exactly where I have placed mine. There can be no deviation from this. Come, we will rehearse a few steps before embarking on our journey through the forest."

Lining us up in a straight row, he began moving forward slowly, looking back over his shoulder to see what we were doing. His footprints were quite large, which made it easy for us to move along safely inside them. But the tension brought on by his intense scrutiny caused one of the girls to stumble and, as another reached out to balance her, their steps veered from the designated path. The Pole exploded in anger.

"If you are going to plod along like clumsy, mindless cattle, I will not even consider this assignment!" he raged.

"Please, please!" the offending girls begged. "We will do better. It is only that we are so nervous—"

"Then we will postpone this journey until you have conquered your nervousness. In your present state, you are sure to be the death of us all."

As he stomped away, still mumbling to himself, I was sure we had lost his services, although I had every intention of approaching him again.

Meanwhile, I talked to the two girls who had stumbled in the line and noticed then that they were both wearing ill-fitting sandals which afforded little or no support. The sandals' threadbare soles made it impossible to avoid sliding around on the icy ground. I knew we had to find them some decent boots to wear.

"We will have to rob two more dead bodies," I told Magda later, when we were alone. "It is essential to the group as a whole. We will go out after dark and check the ditches close to the road. I am sure we will find something there."

Magda's face immediately registered the revulsion she felt. She had learned to accept many things by now, but it was still difficult for her to stomach the thought of robbing the feet of a body that perhaps no longer possessed a head, or one whose blood had been scattered about in an ugly, frozen pattern in the snow. But we both knew that the other girls could not be entrusted with this chore; they would have fainted dead away at the very suggestion of such a thing.

After we had secured the boots and presented them to the girls who were in need, they accepted them without questioning the source. And once they had learned to walk comfortably in them, I returned to the home of the Pole and told him we were ready to make the trip.

"I fear your maternal instincts will be your undoing, Frau Weisberger. You had best leave that pack of clumsy children behind."

"The girls are going with us," I told him flatly. "They have been outfitted with a sturdier pair of shoes and this has done much to improve their balance."

"Very well," the Pole said resignedly. "Tomorrow morning then."

Once we had agreed on the hour, I returned to the girls and told them we had not lost our guide after all. "He has agreed to take us through the forest and will meet us early tomorrow morning, which will give us sufficient time to rehearse the proper method of walking." We did so throughout most of that day, and felt reasonably confident when the appointed hour at last arrived.

It turned out to be an experience much like many others we had known. Its earliest stages, however, were the most frightening. But eventually the soft, crunching snow began to have a lulling affect on our nerves. We followed along in the Pole's footsteps with a disciplined precision that would have made him proud, had he taken the time to notice. But he rarely turned to look at us, having by now resigned himself to the consequences at hand. Occasionally, he would pause and survey the area with a long, questioning glance, which made us fear he had somehow lost his way. But then I saw that he was only checking the location of certain trees and shrubs, obviously relying upon these as landmarks. When he would start moving again, I knew he had recognized certain aspects of the terrain as one would recognize old friends.

After we had been walking for a considerable time, I saw a sight over the Pole's shoulder that seemed too good to be true. Far in the distance, there appeared to be a clearing, and when I was sure that this was what it was, I had to fight the urge to shout with joy. But such an impulsive act would have been more than enough to throw everyone off their stride, so I kept silent and continued to move along.

Then suddenly the Pole stopped so quickly and so unexpectedly that I nearly collided with him.

"What is it?" I whispered.

"Keep still," he said. "There is trouble ahead."

A few moments later, I saw what he meant. Behind a thick clump of trees, I first detected the suggestion of a stealthy movement and then saw the long, gray body of a timber wolf. The animal was thin, almost emaciated and obviously foraging for food. Our lives clearly depended on what direction he took, because even one careless step would be enough to trigger the mines.

As we stood and stared at the animal, he stood and stared at us. The minutes ticked on as our hearts pounded frantically and our limbs turned to stone. Back in the hayloft, I had thought that there could be nothing more unpredictable than a flock of hysterical chickens, but now I saw that the wolf represented a far greater danger. As he began to sniff at the ground and randomly move about, our guide stiffened with fear. Although he said nothing, his rigid stance and stony profile revealed that the wolf was venturing close to a forbidden area.

"Frau Weisberger, have you brought any food with you?" he asked suddenly.

"Some bread and luncheon meats," I told him. "What do you propose to do?"

"If the wolf does not find food, he will continue to search in the snow. Where he is searching now is perilous to us all. Pass me some of what you have, preferably the heel of a loaf, if you have one. The weight of it will make it easier to cast with some accuracy."

"You are going to throw food to the wolf?"

"Yes, in hopes that he will pursue it. I will toss it in a direction away from the mines."

"But what if he is startled by the motion and moves in another direction?"

"Have you anything with a spicy fragrance—salami, perhaps?"

"A little."

"We must take the chance he will follow its scent. Hand me what you have."

I reached inside my coat pocket and broke off a clump of bread, some cheese and some salami. I watched the Pole work it into a tight ball, as the wolf appraised us curiously. As our guide continued to knead the ball of food, the perspiration in his hands began to release some of its aroma. The wolf's long nose tilted upward in the wind, and we knew he had caught the scent. We could see him waiting warily to see what the Pole would do. At last, the man's long arm moved outward and upward, and then I saw the ball of food skipping across the ice-crusted snow in an easterly direction. The famished animal did not hesitate; he loped after this succulent meal as fast as his legs would carry him and the Pole then quickly explained what we would have to do next.

"We must keep him going toward the east. Without moving from your spot, collect whatever rocks are at hand, or make as many snowballs as you can. Then, before he has a chance to move back this way, fire these objects at him with as much force as you can. Be careful that you do not lose your balance in the process."

Once the wolf had swallowed our offering of food, he remained where he was, obviously waiting for a second helping. When none was forthcoming, he took a few tentative steps forward. In a single streak of motion, the Pole drove him back with a few well-aimed stones. Once we saw that the animal was on the defensive, we vowed to keep him there. We all pelted him in turn, until at last the wolf grew confused and discouraged and, sensing the path we wanted him to take, he ambled off in that general direction.

Another eternity passed before we finally reached the clearing, and when we did, we sank to the ground with an overwhelming gratitude that left us weak and trembling. Now that the danger had passed, we dared to fully acknowledge it, and knew that our journey through the forest was nothing short of a miracle. We thanked our guide profusely, realizing the inadequacy of mere words, but he sensed what we were trying to say and assured us that he had been glad to help.

"You all have great courage and determination," he said. "It is my sincere hope you will be reunited with some of your loved ones. You have certainly earned the right to that much."

At this point, we wished each other well and parted company. And so this Pole became yet another of that small invaluable group responsible for helping us find our way.

Had the times not been so chaotic, we might

have thought to collect enough information to stay in touch with these people after the war. But we had little opportunity for that, and so many wonderful, caring friends were lost to us. But while their names and faces would become blurred by the years, their generosity and compassion have never been forgotten.

On the other side of the forest, we encountered several villages that had been devastated by the war. Everywhere we looked, people were scavenging for food, digging down through the layers of snow to reach the frozen fields of potatoes and cabbages underneath. They ate what they found exactly as they found it and, while this was not surprising, it was still a pathetic sight to see.

We walked for several days and eventually reached a small town close to the Slovak border where we spent the night. The next morning, I asked a villager for directions and again was advised of a path that contained many land mines.

"There is another, longer route you can take," he added then. "A much safer one. I will direct you if you are interested."

"By all means!" I said enthusiastically. "Believe me, we are well aware that the shortest way is not always the best. We have had our share of land mines."

As the villager explained everything to me, he said that this alternate route would eventually lead to a railroad station where we might be able to board a freight train to Homona, a city in Slovakia.

We followed his advice and found it to be very good advice indeed. Once we had boarded the train, we immediately felt closer to home.

In Homona, we discovered another Jewish Community Center and availed ourselves of its food and shelter. Before we left, we also received 500 koronas of Czechoslovakian money.

The next morning, we went to the depot and waited for a freight train that was going our way. Five hours later, we learned of one headed for the border town of Chap, located on what had been the Czech-Hungarian border before it fell to the Russians.

Our arrival in Chap gave us a clear indication of what was to come, for it too had been totally bombed out. I knew it was absurd to hope that our own little community had somehow survived intact, but realized now that this is what I had made myself believe, despite much evidence to the contrary.

As if she had read my thoughts, Magda took my hand and patted it gently. "Kralovo Nad Tisza may not be as bad as this. Bombs fall in erratic patterns. You have already seen where one side of a street was completely destroyed while the other side remained untouched."

"That is too much to hope for, my child," I said with a deep sigh. "The fact is, I had thought I was prepared to see our little village in ruins, but now I find that I am not. Let us sit down for a moment.

I do not feel very well."

Sitting by the side of the road, I tried to think of what to do next, for clearly, no further transportation was available.

"We must arrange for a place to stay tonight," I said, after a thoughtful moment or two. "Let us look around and see what we can find."

It was March 12, 1945, a cold, wintry day, no less miserable than many others before it. As the girls and I trudged through the deep snow, we made inquiries here and there, but were unable to find shelter. At long last, we reached a local police station, and were permitted to stay there in order to rest and wait for a train that would take us home.

Late the following afternoon, a military train arrived. When we learned it was traveling to our hometown, we boarded without question and kept to ourselves as we embarked on the last leg of our long journey.

As our destination grew closer and the surrounding area more familiar, my heart began to pound with such accelerated force that I thought it would surely burst in my chest. Finding it hard to breathe, I tried to assume a semi-reclining position, but this only made me feel as if I were strangling, and so I began to shift about until at last Magda noticed my extreme agitation.

"Mama, what is it?" she asked anxiously, and I told her of these wild palpitations that were making me weak and lightheaded.

"It is a case of mind over matter," she said sternly. "You must get hold of yourself. There is nothing wrong with your heart. It is all this anxiety about seeing our village again. Well, if it is gone, it is gone. You must cut your ties with the past. We are alive, and perhaps others will be too. Think of the good things."

As she spoke, I found her droning voice a comfort, like a cool hand on my brow. I listened as she talked of rebuilding our lives, of making up for lost time, of living for the future and burying the past. I could not agree with everything she said, but I listened until her voice became hypnotic, lulling my nerves to sleep and quieting my aching heart.

It was about ten o'clock that night when the train suddenly stopped, and we glanced out to see where we were. I soon recognized the town of Selvus, the place from where we had been shipped to Auschwitz. That alone was enough to revive my anxiety to a new peak. I closed my eyes tightly, but could not blot out the scene of all that suffering and confusion. I relived the separation from other members of the family, felt again the horror of being torn from Bertha, Veronica and baby Lillian. Oh God! If it could be this real after so much time, then surely I was fated to live with that nightmare forever!

"It is all different now," Magda crooned softly. "Look Mama, there are no German soldiers, nothing to fear except your own black thoughts. The war is over, Mama. Everything is over."

I knew in that moment that this child was far more resilient than I. The optimism of youth was always ready to go on, even with only the slightest encouragement. As for me, I was trapped with a thousand memories and sorrows, doomed to drag them along with me wherever I went, seemingly for all time. How wonderful it would be if some overpowering spell of amnesia would suddenly wipe this dreadful slate clean, allowing me to start my life anew as something more than an emotional cripple. Yet, I knew too that some subconscious part of me wanted to remember . . . to remember every intimate detail of this ghastly experience . . . to remember in order to record, and to record in order to what? I could think no further than that, but sensed that there was some long-range purpose in mentally preserving all of this. We survivors were a vital part of history, a chapter in time that could not be lost or forgotten, for that would be tantamount to inviting another holocaust, which would surely happen if the world did not learn from this one.

Perhaps I could begin by writing some of this down. I tried to think of the best way to go about it, how I could even find the time to do it when there would be so much else to do. . . . And as I considered all of this, the hour drew close to midnight, and then suddenly—*we were home!*

When the train stopped, Magda jumped up excitedly, but I found myself unable to move. As she urged me to come, my paralyzed limbs refused to respond and, for a considerable time, I could not even stand. I was overcome with the kind of chills I had often heard malaria victims speak of, and found that my teeth were chattering uncontrollably.

When Magda saw how truly helpless I was, she enlisted the aid of the other girls, and they all supported me as we disembarked from the train.

The station had been cut in two by a bomb and the general atmosphere around the depot was more like a morgue than the hub of activity it had always been.

In the total darkness, only a long ribbon of white was visible, indicating the direction of a snow-covered path. We plodded down this road in silence until at last we came to what had once been Bertha's hotel.

"Mrs. Weisberger owned that place for twenty-five years," I told the girls. "Then it was taken from her and given to a Mr. Fillak. I knew him quite well. Let us see if we can find him."

The girls followed along docilely as I entered the front yard, walked up to the house and timidly knocked on the door. When there was no answer, I knocked harder, and waited for some sound of movement inside. There was none.

"He is gone. Or dead," I said, with a sudden crack in my voice.

As we continued down the road, we all began to cry. Every mood was highly contagious now. Had any one of us broken out in hysterical laughter, all the others would soon have too.

"We will go to my house," I said then. In my mind's eye, it still existed as a haven against every storm. I tried not to think of it the way it had been, but since that was my last recollection of it, I could hardly see it any other way. When at last we arrived there, I looked at this apparition in the night and tried to equate it with the house in which I had lived for nineteen years.

All of the doors and windowpanes were gone, the steps were splintered and broken, and the wind stirred huge drifts of snow through its stark, empty shell. As my imagination ran rampant, I could see the invaders assaulting this house, stripping it bare with their vulturous appetites, laying waste its quiet dignity, its very identity. Now it could have been anyone's house. There was no hint of those who had once lived there, of the joyful events that had occurred inside its walls, and the shared love of its inhabitants. No, now it was anyone's house–or no one's. Having been trampled on by so many, it no longer had anyone's stamp upon it. I looked at it for a long time and cried, mourning its loss, and the way it had been destroyed.

"I will never forgive the Germans for this!" I cried out, through gritted teeth. "This senseless slaughter and destruction must be avenged. It must be avenged!"

At that moment, I felt Magda tugging at my arm, and glanced down to see her gaunt, shivering form beside me. "What of Mrs. Fiksler?" she asked, reminding me of a Russian woman who had lived only a few doors away.

"We will try," I said listlessly, for by now I was sure that the entire village was a ghost town.

When we reached the Fiksler house, I went to the door and gave a brisk knock. Much to my surprise, the door was opened by Mrs. Fiksler herself. For a moment, I could not speak and, as the woman began to regard me suspiciously, I clutched her arm and said, "Don't you recognize me? Don't you know me, Mrs. Fiksler? I am Mrs. Weisberger, your neighbor."

The woman's eyes widened endlessly, and then she hugged me to her as she said over and over, "Oh God, it is true, it is true, it is true!" When she told me to come in, I explained that Magda and some other girls were waiting in the yard, and she immediately called out that they should all come inside. Frozen to the bone, the girls eagerly complied.

Once inside, we were greeted by a couple of Russian soldiers playing cards at the table. After we had been given something to eat, we sat and discussed the tragedies of the war, as they applied to us.

Mrs. Fiksler had married a Jewish man during the First World War and he had brought her to our village afterward. They had enjoyed a happy life together until he was taken away to the concentration camps.

"I know he will not return," she said, with an air of resignation. "His age was against him. Unless he escaped, there is no way that he could have survived."

"Well, we can hope for the best, but having been there, I cannot give you much encouragement," I said. "Concentration camps are difficult, if not impossible to escape from. Still, I have heard of a few who managed it, and perhaps your husband was among them."

We kept our conversation as optimistic as possible, although we remained realistic in our expectations.

"Magda and I have also hoped and prayed for the survival of some of our family members," I said, "although we have every reason to believe that they are all lost to us."

"Then you do not know that your nephew, Joseph Kraus, came back? And his boyhood friend, Tibor Weis?"

I stared at Mrs. Fiksler in total amazement. "Margaret's son is alive? Are you sure?" I asked, hardly daring to believe her words.

"Yes, it is true. He is staying in Bertha Weisberger's house. He and several other survivors."

"But how can that be? We went there first and knocked and knocked, but no one answered."

"Well, they are there all the same. Perhaps they did not answer because they thought you were soldiers. Tomorrow morning, we will let them know you are here. Now, you had better get some sleep, along with the rest of us."

At this point, I suggested we make our beds on the floor. "We are used to it," I explained. "Just a simple blanket will do."

"What nonsense!" Mrs. Fiksler retorted. "You have been through enough of that sort of thing. You will sleep in nice clean beds after your long, difficult journey. I can think of no one who is more entitled to a little comfort."

Since she did not understand the real reason for my hesitation, I had no choice but to tell her. It embarrassed me to speak in front of the Russian soldiers since I considered this a somewhat indelicate subject.

"The truth is, we are unclean. Our bodies are covered with lice, and until we have had an opportunity to fumigate ourselves, it would be best if we slept on the floor."

"That is of no consequence," Mrs. Fiksler insisted and, in the end, she had her way. That night, we slept in our own town, in warm, comfortable beds, reassured by this woman's kind and gentle ways.

8

The next morning, we awoke to a mad confusion in the house. As I lay perfectly still, trying to make some sense of it, I heard the voice of my nephew, Joseph Kraus. There could be no mistake about it! Over the voices of several others, I heard his own and then a rousing wave of laughter.

"Quick, Magda, we must get downstairs!" I said. "Mrs. Fiksler has gone and brought Joe. He is here—in the house!"

We scurried about excitedly, trying to make ourselves presentable, although we clearly hadn't the patience or even the time for that. It would take days of boiling our clothes and blankets just to rid ourselves of the lice, and after that only a regular diet of decent food and some better clothes would make us look human again.

As we came into the kitchen where Joe and his

friends were gathered around the table, he stood up slowly and looked at us as if he were seeing two ghosts. I suppose we must have looked at him in much the same way and, for a long moment, we all stood where we were, trying to adjust to the miracle of one another's survival. As his eyes drank us in, he cocked his head slightly, almost as if he were trying to see behind us. Then I knew he had continued to hope that somehow his mother had also survived. As I ran toward him, I was overpowered by certain conflicting emotions: the joy of being reunited with someone so dear, and the knowledge he would have to be told about Margaret.

A cry of joy lodged in my throat, became a sob and then welled over into waves of tears and laughter. We held each other for a long time, not really daring to let go, afraid this miracle of reunion might yet fade and die. And then, all at once, an incredible thing happened. I could feel a new current of strength and courage passing from him to me like a life-giving transfusion, and my heart welled over with love and gratitude.

"You look wonderful!" Joe shouted enthusiastically, which caused us to laugh uproariously since we knew only too well how we looked.

"It is a miracle!" I said, still clinging to his hand. "I had given up hope...."

As my own emotions overwhelmed me, Joe hugged me to him and said, "Even when I'd given up hoping, I never gave up praying. I am sure the same was true for you."

I considered this as Joe, Magda and I stood huddled together in Mrs. Fiksler's warm, fragrant kitchen.

"You will come and stay with us in Grandmother's house," Joe was saying when I next took the time to listen. "Now, eat the breakfast Mrs. Fiksler has prepared for you, and then get your things."

We did as we were told, happy to have someone else take charge of our lives for a while. After so much frantic plotting and scheming, I felt as if I did not want to assume the responsibility of another independent decision for a long time to come.

After Magda and I had gathered our meager belongings, we thanked Mrs. Fiksler for taking us in and then, along with the other girls in our party, followed Joe back to the Weisberger house. There we attempted to work out the best accommodations for everyone. Once again, I suggested the girls be given any available beds since Magda and I were used to sleeping on the floor.

"I don't doubt that *all* of you are used to sleeping on the floor," Joe said, "but you have seen the last of that kind of life."

"You don't understand," I whispered to him then. "It embarrasses me to tell you this, but Magda and I are both infested with lice."

Taking note of my hesitant confession of this humiliating fact, Joe burst into gales of laughter.

"You tell me this as if I did not know of such things? My dear, you could not surprise me with anything you said. Do not concern yourself with these unfortunate by-products of the war. They can be washed away more easily than the pain and suffering we have known."

I knew, too, that there was more pain and suffering to come, because the subject of Joe's mother could not be avoided much longer. The questioning look never left his eyes, and soon after the other girls in our party had set out on their own journey home, I knew the time had come.

We sat together in the parlor and discussed the very admirable way in which Joe had been able to reorganize his life. Upon returning to Bertha's house, I had been surprised to find he had established a small tailoring business, and that he already had several customers.

"How did you manage it?" I asked. "The furniture and the sewing machine! Why, things look almost normal in this room."

"It lacks a woman's touch," Joe said, with a coy smile. "I have no talent for such things. But it was necessary to begin working again. Not only for all the obvious reasons, but to keep from thinking, too."

"Yes . . . work is therapy," I agreed, and then gazed thoughtfully out the window.

"Aunt Shari, I must ask. Is there anything you can tell me about Mama? Was she with you? Did you spend any time together?"

"Yes . . . in the beginning. When we first went to Auschwitz, Magda, Margaret and I were together."

"And . . . ?"

"It was very difficult for your mother, Joe. She was a very refined and sensitive soul, and she was deeply repulsed by the horror of that dreadful place."

"I'm sure it was no less agonizing for you."

"Yes, but in a different way. Magda and I hated what we saw and what we were forced to live with. But we lived with it and adapted to it in a way Margaret could not seem to do. We begged her to eat the rotten food, to take no notice of how it looked or what it tasted like, and to think only in terms of survival. She found these suggestions utterly distasteful, but perhaps that is because I did not put them to her in the proper way. And each day, she saw us becoming more animal-like in our habits and attitudes, and mourned the loss of what had been beauty and dignity in this world. To a certain extent, we all felt something of that, but your mother felt it more. It took its toll on her, and in a way that seemed irreversible. But in time I began to realize that the quality of our lifestyle was not the real problem."

Joe gave a long, audible sigh. "I thought you were going to tell me she died of starvation," he said.

"No," I told him. "Your mother did not starve."

I could feel his eyes upon me as I paused and tried to organize my thoughts.

"Did you get separated then?" he asked. "You mentioned that you and Magda were sent to a work camp. Is that when you were separated?"

"No . . . it was before that. You see, after Bertha, Veronica and Lillian were taken from us, Margaret came to the conclusion that they had been taken to a special place, somewhere where only older people and very young children were kept. At the time, it seemed pointless to destroy her illusion, for there did not seem to be any harm in it."

"But then . . . ?"

"But then it began to dominate her thoughts in a way we did not even suspect. She became extremely reclusive, keeping to her bunk and seldom talking to anyone. We had no way of knowing what she planned to do."

"Oh God, I think I know what you are going to tell me!" Joe said, and began to pace back and forth with great agitation. "She tried to escape and was shot by the guards."

"No, no."

"Then she must have tried to scale the fence and electrocuted herself."

"No, nothing like that happened."

"Are you telling me she is still alive, that somewhere *she still lives?* How is that possible? How did she manage it?"

The strain of continually misleading him through my awkward explanations greatly complicated the task of telling him the truth. But having come this far, I knew I would have to finish what I had started.

"Joe, please sit down, and let me tell you what I have to say. I am telling this badly, but I do not intend to mislead you further."

He did as I asked, and stared at me silently as I gathered the strength to continue.

"As time went on," I told him, "your mother became obsessed with an idea of her own. Feeling that Bertha was too old to care for children as young as my littlest ones, and believing she was needed to help care for them, she began to talk about going to them. Whenever she spoke in this way, we could not bring ourselves to tell her where they had been taken, but warned her to keep such thoughts to herself. The daily roll calls were a nerve-wracking experience for us, because we could never be sure what she might say or do."

"Are you saying she had begun to lose touch with reality? That her mind was affected?"

"Whose mind was *not* affected!" I argued in Margaret's behalf. "The strange little things she would say and do . . . well, she was not alone in developing these little quirks. There were many in our group who exhibited extremely odd behavior."

"Still, her condition must have been worse than the others—I feel there is something you are not telling me."

"Yes, in time she became worse than the rest. But we always kept an eye on her, and did what we could to protect her. But then . . . one morning, at the end of roll call, she suddenly stepped forward and insisted she be allowed to go with the others who had been taken from the lines. She did not know the fate of those people. She thought they were being taken to another camp, where Bertha and the children were being housed."

"I see," Joe said quietly. "And I suppose those bastard Germans were happy to oblige."

"Oh yes. Unfortunately, the situation was not what it was on those two occasions when I was able to keep Magda from being taken away. The same opportunities did not exist, but even if they had, Margaret herself would have fought my efforts to save her."

"Yes, yes, I understand," Joe said, and slowly moved out of the room. I made no effort to follow him, knowing he needed some time alone to reconcile himself to the truth. In his own mind, his mother had not been totally lost until now. But now there was nothing more to hope for. My words had put an end to the possibility of a miracle, and destroyed in him the last shred of optimism.

I would have understood if his black mood had continued for days or even weeks, but not long after we had finished speaking, I heard the gentle whirring of the sewing machine, and found him working as diligently as before, with a look of grim determination on his face.

"May I help you in any way?" I asked, leaving him to decide upon my actual meaning.

"No," he said quietly. "I am nearly done."

"Your garments have not lost their touch of elegance," I said, as I ran my fingers across the lapel of a hand-tailored coat. "It is still there, despite the inferior cloth, and the questionable abilities of that machine. I know it was not designed for commercial use, but you seem to have convinced it that it is capable of doing the very finest work."

"The machine skips now and again—a most annoying habit," Joe said. "But after all, it is a victim of the war, even as we are. It is difficult to find anything that functions well these days. I am grateful the machine works at all."

"Do you think we will ever again know a time when elegance is the order of the day? When people complement their wardrobes with such fine accessories as soft leather gloves, and silk top hats, and take such things for granted, as they once did?"

"Sooner than you think," Joe said. "There are many who are not accustomed to being deprived. They have a habit of making their desires known. After that, it all comes back to the law of supply and demand."

"I have nothing but contempt for such people!" I said angrily. "I've already heard some of their complaints. How persecuted they feel because they must endure the shortage of certain things. I wish them all a hundred years in Auschwitz. That should bring their priorities back into focus."

"Perhaps. But then again, I was able to enjoy

certain advantages because of their greed, even as you were."

"What do you mean?" I asked curiously.

"The last furlough I was given from the forced labor camp was granted after I had finished a suit for one of the high officers in charge of the encampment. Off and on, my tailoring skills proved highly beneficial, just as yours did. But they would have had no value at all if the most undeserving among us had not insisted upon having those things to which they were not entitled."

"I suppose that's true," I said. "But we paid dearly for every scrap of food we put into our mouths. And I am sure the same was true for you."

"Yes, it was hard," Joe admitted. "In the month of October, they sent us to work on a building that was never completed. While we were working on it, we were also required to live there. It was to have been an officers' headquarters, but throughout the war it remained an empty hulk, with concrete floors and no doors or windows. The wind and snow blew through that place with a bitter force that many did not survive. A stove had been built into the center of one room, but without the proper connections or anything with which to fuel it, it remained useless. As a joke, we placed a candle inside and pretended to use this for warmth."

"What were you given to eat?"

"Black coffee in the morning, a ladle of soup for lunch, and another ladle of soup and some dry bread for supper. It was not a diet that sustained one for any great length of time, and so we were frequently punished for falling behind schedule."

"How did they punish you?"

"In various ways. One form of punishment was referred to as a 'Conditioning Program.' It was just a lot of rigorous marching and running. And for those who could not keep up, there were other disciplinary measures. Sometimes the unfortunate ones were suspended from a tree after a long rope had been looped under their arms and their hands had been tied behind their backs. Once a victim's circulation had been cut off, he would generally faint. When this happened, he was taken down, revived with cold water, and then suspended again. This game would continue for as long as it provided any amusement for the officers."

"I will never forgive the Germans for these cruel and inhuman acts!" I said then. "I could match every story you have told me with gruesome tales of my own, but more important than the telling is the remembering. I shall never, never forget what has been done to us, nor will I allow any surviving member of my family, or even their children's children, to forget."

"Yes, I know how you feel, and I agree," Joe replied. "Still, it was not the German soldiers who did these things to us. It was the Hungarians—the Hungarians who believed the promises Hitler had made to them and who turned against their own people in the name of personal profit."

"Well, they have all reaped the profit they deserve," I said. "They have gone down in total and humiliating defeat. Their dream of power is ended. But you haven't told me how it ended for you, Joe, how you were able to make it back home."

"I escaped from the camp," he explained. "And in those final days, it was not difficult to remain inconspicuous. Taking advantage of all that chaos and confusion, I traveled throughout the day and sought refuge in barns and other abandoned buildings at night. My methods were not unlike your own—and fortunately, were as successful."

As he spoke, I looked out the window and saw only Russian soldiers milling about in the streets. Since arriving home, I had tried to reacquaint myself with this community, to adopt it once again as my own village. But it bore no resemblance to that place, seeming more like a cemetery.

Of the 700 Jewish people who had once lived there, only thirty-five had returned and these were all young boys and girls, except for one other married woman like myself and an older man.

As long as the Russians remained in our village, they continued their looting. They were particularly fond of wristwatches, and would tear them from the arms of their owners in cases where the watches were not relinquished voluntarily. The Russians were exceptionally abrasive toward the Hungarians, whom they now considered Nazi collaborators. In cases where I knew this was true, I found I was no less vindictive and was quick to report these people to the Russian Commandant.

But I rarely ventured out into the streets, for the climate there was extremely unsettling. Many of the residents were bitter about the destruction in their village and blamed the Jews for what had happened. I could not trust myself to be around these people, since their tasteless remarks were enough to make me want to fly for their throats.

As the weeks passed, I became increasingly restless. It seemed I should be doing something more than merely existing. And as I began to gain strength, I grew more ambitious and began to look about for something to do.

In order to accommodate the large numbers of people who were regularly arriving by train, Joe finally suggested we open up a combination bar and restaurant.

"Well, I can certainly see the need," I said, "but there would also be certain complications. I mean, to properly run such an establishment, we would need fixtures and—"

"The fixtures will be less of a problem than the food and liquor supplies. We can confiscate chairs, tables and countertops from the old abandoned buildings that *used* to be restaurants and bars. Some of their furniture inventory has remained intact."

"And what about the location? Have you decided where the best site would be?"

"My friend Tibor can help us there. You may

remember that his parents owned a large apartment across from the railroad station. At one time, it also housed a barber shop, restaurant and drugstore. The restaurant and drugstore were owned by Jewish people. It would be an ideal place to start again."

"Well, I can see that you and your friend Tibor have given all of this careful thought. I must say the idea appeals to me, Joe. I am becoming extremely restless and eager to do something. But where will we get enough food and liquor for our needs?"

"From neighboring towns and villages. Some of them weren't as badly damaged as ours. And we've also learned the whereabouts of certain moonshiners—"

"Moonshiners?!"

Joe laughed at my shocked tone of voice. "Yes. You needn't worry, Aunt Shari. What they will supply us with is of sufficient quality for the Russians to drink. They seem to have cast-iron stomachs. And the less daring among our patrons can settle for some home brew or a glass of the fermented grape."

"Well, that leaves only the dinner menu to think about," I said. "I suppose it will be easier to get potatoes than anything else. Perhaps I shall make a large pot of potato soup. I would like to have something more festive for our opening day, but we are limited to what is available."

"I have tasted your potato soup," Joe said with

a sharp twinkle in his eye. "I can assure you it will be much more than our patrons expect!"

There seemed to be some truth in what he said, because during our first day of operation I watched as the customers eagerly consumed their bowls of thick, steaming soup. By noon it was all gone, along with five liters of whiskey. We had made a good profit for the day, and closed our doors several hours prematurely.

The next day we were prepared for a second crowd of people with *ten* liters of whiskey, *two* pots of soup and three dozen hard-boiled eggs. The travelers from the train made short work of it all. They were so hungry that they were begging to buy food at any price. We had to remind them of the shortages. We would gladly have supplied them with additional things to eat if we had only had them.

In time, our situation improved, and we were able to obtain small cuts of beef and pork. From these, I prepared delicious meals that caused many customers to abandon their table manners and enthusiastically smack their lips and lick their fingers.

Magda and I were no less avid about food than our patrons, since we ate sizable portions of everything we cooked. We were bottomless pits after such a long period of starvation. In time, I was even inclined to make a joke of it.

"If it doesn't eat us," I would say, "we'll eat it."

Some of our gentile neighbors, taking notice of

the success of our business, decided to compete with us. But they did not prosper nearly as well as we did, and were altogether unsuccessful in luring away our faithful following.

On May 9, 1945, the war ended. Soon after that, the military trains started coming in. Two or three trainloads arrived daily, and our village was nearly overrun with Russian soldiers—all demanding liquor to drink. Their breed was difficult enough to manage under normal circumstances, but once under the fiery influence of intoxicating spirits, their behavior became extremely riotous.

They would come through our doors in droves of thirty or forty, demanding vodka at the top of their lungs. The first time this happened to Magda, she had never heard the word before and totally misunderstood their request. But since it bore a close resemblance in sound to *wasser,* the German word for water, that was what she served them. Downing the clear liquid in a single gulp, one Russian's face was the picture of confusion and ultimate disgust as he spat upon the bar and threatened to inflict bodily injury upon this poor girl for playing such a nasty trick on him. As Magda ran from the room in terror, it became obvious that the soldier was more disturbed with the uproarious laughter of his companion than he was at having been served a glass of water.

As a result of this incident, we soon learned what vodka was and made a practice of keeping it in stock. The Russians paid us in rubles and

German marks and occasionally would also trade for fine fabrics they had brought from Germany, or exquisite pieces of jewelry. In time, we realized they were willing to trade anything they had for vodka, which they drank from huge water glasses filled to the brim.

By the end of May, we began to see a ragged influx of Jewish refugees, young boys and girls who had managed to survive and now returned to find that everything and everyone else was gone. A community kitchen was established in the middle of town to accommodate their immediate needs. It was run by a good-hearted fellow named Morris Zelmanovitz, who had also lost everything in the war.

Early in the month of June, we were visited by Isidor Grunberg, a family friend who was to tell us an incredible piece of news.

"I met your husband in Austria in March, Mrs. Weisberger," he said. "He was in good condition at the time. I cannot tell you any more than that, but still there is reason to hope."

Magda, who had overheard our conversation, began jumping about for joy.

"Papa is alive! He is alive! I know it!" she cried and, in that moment, it was impossible to doubt it. As she and I danced around the room, we began to make plans about how we would welcome him, since we now could surprise him with something more than our own survival. We had a fine, thriving business, having successfully established ourselves in the community.

"He will never expect all this!" I said excitedly. "He will have time to recuperate from the effects of the war and not have to immediately concern himself with earning a living."

"We must have a party, Mama!" Magda insisted. "But not just a party, a feast! A feast of all the finest foods we can find. He must have the best of everything to make him well and strong again!"

As the days passed, our original plans were greatly embellished as we considered first one thing and then another to ensure the happiest homecoming possible for Solomon Weisberger. Oh God, what a joyous day—there could never be another like it!

We had been through so much, but we could still have a good life together. For the first time in a long while, I allowed myself to consider such a possibility.

Eventually, we would have to leave this little village and travel to a land that offered far greater opportunity: America! It would be a new beginning with new hope and promise. There was nothing more for us here.

From that point on, we lived in a state of constant expectancy, which was no easy matter, since we had long since overtaxed our minds and bodies. Each time another small group of refugees came straggling home, I would scrutinize their faces with an intensity borne of desperation.

As hope continued to flicker and wane, Magda

and I attempted to bolster one another's spirits by speaking of Sol's return as if it were inevitable.

"Who can say what means of transportation is available to him, if any," I would point out with a deep sigh, remembering our own difficult journey home. "If he is on foot much of the time, his progress will be slow."

Even so, I held a clear picture in my mind of his slow, steady progress. I knew that if he lived, he would have to satisfy his own curiosity about family survivors, just as we had, before he could go on to anything else.

And then, one day, we received a highly encouraging sign in the arrival of Olga Weisberger, the twenty-four-year-old daughter of my husband's older brother, Ignatz. Seeing her was like receiving some confirmation of my own husband's survival, even though there was no real logic in this thought. After Olga came to live with us, she maintained a vigil for her father, her mother, Rella, and a brother, Otto, in the same intense way we continued to hold out some hope for Sol, and even my younger sister, Blanche Klein. I had never been entirely certain of her fate—not as certain as I was of the fate of Bertha, Veronica and baby Lillian. Blanche had been considered a sturdy specimen by the Germans. It was altogether possible she had been utilized in the war effort, which could have been her key to survival, as it had been ours.

As spring made way for summer, we spoke less

optimistically about the possibility of anyone's return, but the fires of hope refused to die. At times, I damned their very existence, for it seemed that my foolish expectations were always doomed to crash against the rocks of some grim reality.

As the summer moved on, I became so finely attuned to the arrival of new refugees in the community that I sensed their presence even before I saw them. As they moved along the road, I often saw my husband in the gait of someone's walk, in a certain slant of the shoulders or in the elusive angle of a profile. I knew my imagination had been overworked to the point of playing tricks on me, but still I could not keep from seeing Sol. He was the one I longed to see above all others, and so my mind would periodically conjure up a vision of him, as if to satisfy my wishes in some vicarious way.

And then one day, yet another refugee entered the restaurant, a gentleman we recognized as Sam Farkas, a friend and neighbor of many years. He looked gaunt and wasted inside his ragged clothes, suggesting something more debilitating than the laborious life of a concentration camp.

"It was the typhoid. . . . " he muttered in a weak, cracking voice. "With little or no medication, and the unclean conditions in which we were forced to live, it soon reached epidemic proportions."

I watched him lift a spoon to his lips and fought the urge to reach out and steady his hand as the hot liquid splashed on the countertop. He was so frail and sickly that he could barely feed himself. For a while, I left him to the task of consuming his simple meal, although my mind was burning with the possibility that he might know something of Sol. At long last, I could no longer contain myself. Bringing Sam a plate of steaming, boiled potatoes, I refilled his soup bowl and asked him the inevitable question.

"I don't wish to burden you with endless inquiries and painful memories of the past but, Sam, I must ask you this. Do you know anything of my beloved Sol? Some months ago, I learned through another party that he had been seen in Austria, and that he seemed well at the time. Is it possible you could add anything to that? I continue to hope and pray he will return to us. The constant uncertainty is agonizing!"

Sam Farkas stirred his soup thoughtfully for a moment, shaking his head slowly from side to side. "Yes, not knowing is often worse than knowing the truth."

"W-What do you mean?" I asked hesitantly.

"Only that facts can be painful, but an absence of facts is a wretched business also."

"Sam, is there something you know—something you can tell me?"

"That is why I came," he said in a low, somber tone. "To put an end to your uncertainties. I was liberated with your husband and remained with him throughout the typhoid siege. He contracted it along with myself. We were all in very bad condition, weakened as we were from lack of food and hard work. We were placed in a makeshift hospital in Wels, Austria."

"Yes, yes! That coincides with what Isidor Grunberg told us. Except that he said Sol looked well. Apparently he managed to recuperate then, just as you did."

Sam laughed bitterly. "I am not yet recuperated, Frau Weisberger. Far from it. I am sure you can appreciate that typhoid fever takes its toll when anyone who is already weak and starving becomes afflicted with it."

"Yes, it is a miracle to come through such a thing," I said, as I urged him to put more gravy on his potatoes.

"Thank you," he muttered, as he quietly declined my offer. "It is difficult for me to eat very much at one time. It takes a while for the system to readjust to normal portions of food."

"Tell me what happened when you and my husband left the hospital. Did you—"

"You misunderstand!" Sam Farkas said sadly. "I spent many hours with your husband. In our conversations, he shared his feelings and fears. 'I have no one to live for,' he told me. 'My wife, Shari, had a baby, and we both know that mothers and babies were sent straight to the gas chambers. My two-year-old Lillian, my seven-year-old Veronica, surely they had no chance. My oldest daughter, Magda, was a frail girl of fifteen who was not capable of the hard labor Germany needed. As you can see,' Solomon Weisberger told me, 'they must all have perished.' " Sam Farkas hesitated, as if to draw from some reserve of energy.

"We did not leave together," he continued wearily. "If Isidor Grunberg saw your husband, apparently he saw him before he was stricken with typhoid. I regret to tell you this, Frau Weisberger, but your husband succumbed to the disease. I personally witnessed his death in the hospital."

The initial shock of this news left me totally numb. "Thank you for telling me," I mumbled finally, and backed away from the counter. I continued to walk backward as if recoiling from the news, until at last I stumbled into Magda in the small kitchen.

"Mama, what is it?" she asked, noticing my stricken face. "What has happened?"

"I-It's about your father," I told her. "Sam Farkas tells me he was with him in Wels, Austria. . . . "

"Yes? Yes? And what else? Oh Mama, is it bad news?"

"The worst. Your father died in the hospital of typhoid fever. He isn't coming home, precious child. He is gone—with the others. Our waiting is finally over."

For the balance of the day, we were of no use to ourselves or to anyone else. After months of watching and waiting for this beloved member of our family who had come so close to finding his way back to us, I could not accept the cruel twist of fate that had now snatched him away forever.

After several hours of hysterical behavior, I adamantly announced to my business partners and my daughter that the time had certainly come to leave this wretched place, and that I would not rest until we had begun a new life in America.

"Everything here reeks of misery and more misery! There will never be an end to it. Nothing good can ever happen here. It has become a place where even our own neighbors have turned against us. In some bizarre way, they blame us for everything that has happened, as if we were actually capable of perpetrating such horrendous acts against our own people, somehow encouraging this mindless cruelty and violence that has cost us everything and everyone. How could we possibly be responsible for such a thing? I'm tired of being blamed! And hated! And persecuted! I will not stay here another day. Not another hour. Not another minute!"

As Joe Kraus and Tibor moved forward to quiet or steady me, I ran from the restaurant and out into the street. Giving no thought to directions, I ran along the main thoroughfare of town, as if I were being pursued. Had anyone asked why I was running, I could not have told them, although a psychiatrist might have sensed that I was running away from the end of everything. My life here was over, every possibility for personal happiness was gone . . . there seemed to be no purpose in living. Everything had been buried along with my beloved husband, whose only crime on earth had been to love and care for his family, and to drive himself to the point of exhaustion and, ultimately, to a premature death. I could not imagine a life without him. Whatever I had been telling myself up until now—that I could endure, persevere and continue on because that is what he would have wanted—was a lie. In that moment, I wanted nothing more than to rest beside him, to let all the madness in this world go on without me.

Moving along through the numbing fog of my own grief, I glanced about suddenly, as if to get my bearings. I saw another woman moving toward me with a slow, ambling gait. There was nothing familiar about her, and yet she struck me as an odd caricature of myself. For a long moment, I could not place the resemblance—not until I recognized the style and pattern of her dress. Then, all at once I knew. I knew this garment was one that had once been part of my own wardrobe, a dress I had made for myself for some special occasion.

When the woman moved to pass me on the road, I detained her with a quick, light touch. "How lovely you look in that dress," I said, with a deadly calm. "One rarely sees well-dressed people these days."

"W-What?" the woman asked sharply, and then glancing down at the garment, she stroked it with quick, nervous gestures. "Oh, this dress. Why, thank you. I'm glad you like it."

I gripped her wrist as she sought to move away.

"The detail work is so delicate and fine. Not at all like anything you would find in a store. Tell me, is it hand-tailored?"

"N-No. That is, I don't know. I really have to go now."

"Where did you get it?" I persisted, refusing to release my hold on her.

The woman's face suddenly became flushed with anger. "I really don't see what business it is of yours!" With that she tried to push me aside, but I grabbed her arm and quickly spun her around.

"Oh, but it *is* my business, you rotten thief! You stole that dress from my house along with whatever else looked good to you at the time. Life has been very easy for you, hasn't it? Once we were herded away, it no longer mattered that we had once been neighbors, or that we once enjoyed the same amount of respect and acceptance in this community. We weren't supposed to complicate your miserable existence by coming back to witness your greed and reclaim our belongings. Well, as it happens, I *have* come back, and I *am* reclaiming what is mine—starting with this dress!"

With a swift, violent motion, I clutched the dress at the neckline and tore it from the frightened woman's body. As she screamed and tried to cover herself, a small crowd began to gather, but no one moved to intervene. In that moment, I felt capable of killing them all, and there must have been something in my eyes that told them as much.

Standing over the cowering woman, I tore the dress to shreds and watched the ragged remnants flutter away on a breeze. Satisfied that the garment could be of no further use to her, I walked away as her hysteria began to build.

"She's crazy! A madwoman!" I heard her cry, and I thought this description not an altogether inaccurate analysis of my current state of mind. Perhaps I could not accomplish it all in one day, but I vowed to get away from these people, this town and its grim reminders of the past. I had one daughter left, one person to carve out a future for. She did not deserve to grow up in an atmosphere of hatred and bigotry. For a long time, we had been hated simply because we lived. It was time to put an end to all that. Otherwise, no decent life was possible.

As my obsession with America continued to grow, I became less talkative on the subject. I could see that I had startled Joe, Tibor and even Magda with my recent ravings. and suffered their concerned glances for a long time afterward.

I continued to operate the business, but without ambition or any real sense of accomplishment. I began to wrack my brain for a plan that would take us away to a new land and a new beginning. I knew, however, this could only be accomplished if I somehow managed to reach one of my two sisters in America. Since all of my personal belongings had been lost, I no longer had a record of their addresses, although I remembered that my sister

Pearl, Mrs. Louis Stein, lived in Philadelphia, and Sarah, Mrs. Sam Machlovitz, resided in Chicago.

"I must think of a way to reach them!" I repeatedly said to Magda, who could see no way to calm my spirits except one.

"Perhaps if we wait a little longer," she said, "Aunt Blanche will also return. By then, you may recall the address in Philadelphia or Chicago, and then we can all go together."

I had tried to put the matter of Blanche out of my mind, not wishing to give myself false hopes as I had done with my husband. But the possibility of her survival could not be ruled out altogether, and so I continued to hope, without really admitting to myself that this was what I was doing.

And then, one day, a woman from a neighboring village came to see me, and resolved the matter for all time.

"Blanche made the mistake of stealing some potatoes from a wagon," she told me. "This angered an officer close at hand who picked up a rock and struck her in the head with it. Under ordinary circumstances, it might have been considered a superficial wound, but as it was, it became seriously infected and I am sorry to say, eventually cost Blanche her life."

"Can it be? Can this really be?" I wailed in utter despair. To think she had survived so much only to be cut down by a rock to the head!

"I fear it is true," the woman said, "because I was with her at the end. She told me that if she did not survive, I was to come back and inform you where she had hidden certain valuables."

After the woman had gone, I fell into yet another state of deep despondency which only increased my determination to reach some family member in America.

"Imagine that you are writing to them," Magda suggested, "and that you have the envelopes in front of you. If you can picture that scene, perhaps you can remember the addresses."

Although I played this mental game throughout the day and half the night, I was not rewarded with the answers I sought.

And then one night, as I lay tossing and turning in my bed, I suddenly saw the address of the sister in Philadelphia as clearly as if a giant hand had written it across the ceiling of my room:

> 111 Allegheny Avenue
> Philadelphia, Pennsylvania.

The next morning, I scribbled out a brief note and gave it to a Russian Jewish officer to take with him to Prague. He promised to mail the letter from there. Some four weeks later, I knew he had been as good as his word for that was when an answer came.

My sister's telegram advised that they were taking immediate steps to bring us to America and, with that news, my normally buoyant spirits returned.

But other complications were under way. The Russians had started to close the borders, and each passing day brought us deeper into the shadow of the Iron Curtain. With many things still to attend to, I once again fell victim to my old anxieties.

Meanwhile, the operation of the business became more of a burden than a blessing as the Russian soldiers began to impose themselves upon us in a way that threatened our very welfare. Their drunken revelry had long since passed the stage where it could be safely tolerated and finally culminated in an incident that eventually convinced us to close the place down.

On that particular occasion, we had closed early in the day because of a short supply of food and drink. While the majority of our patrons were reasonably resigned to these unpredictable hours, the Russians were less inclined to accept circumstances over which we had no control. Having arrived at our door one evening only to find it locked, they began to shout in wild, abusive language and demanded they be allowed to enter.

"They're all drunk!" Magda whispered in a voice that trembled with fear. "Oh God, Mama, this time they're going to break the door down. I just know it!"

"Well, we won't be here when they do," I told her, and quickly herded her out the back, explaining to Joe that we would seek safety at the house of a neighbor.

"Very well, but I don't intend to let it go at that," Joe retorted angrily. "They must be made to understand they cannot behave in this manner and get by with it. Be on your way, and I will go for the police."

This frightening incident would prove to have its share of comic relief, although we would not know this until much later, when at last Joe reappeared, in such a state of disarray that we could only stare at him in amazement. That evening, he had been wearing his best suit, which had been hand-tailored from fine cloth he himself had designed and made. Now it was matted to his body and covered with a thick slime that emitted such a stench that it was difficult to tolerate his presence.

"What in the world has happened to you?" I asked. I listened as he offered his explanation from the porch rather than coming in and soiling the flooring of the house.

"I was trying to avoid being seen by the Russians as I left the restaurant," he explained, "and in the course of selecting the darkest path, I failed to see the cesspool until I had fallen into it."

"You fell in the cesspool?" I whooped, not knowing whether to laugh or cry, because his suit appeared to be ruined, and I could see that his spirits were severely dampened as well.

Overhearing our conversation, Magda went to the kitchen and came back with a large pail of water. "Stay outside," she instructed, "and I will rinse you off."

Grabbing another pail, I was quick to join her, and so we took turns, dousing Joe with pails of water from the well until at last most of the vile-smelling residue had been washed away.

Not until he had had an opportunity to properly cleanse himself and change into fresh clothing did we allow ourselves to see the humor in the situation.

"I suppose the suit is ruined," I said, trying hard not to laugh, although Joe now seemed no less amused than I.

"In these times, no suit can afford to be ruined," he said with a good-natured grin. "As soon as I can bear to get near it, I will rejuvenate it somehow."

"You'll need a gas mask to get near it," Magda volunteered then, and this was enough to send us into a second round of laughter.

"But one thing we seem to have forgotten through all this," I said at last, "is the Russians. Since you weren't able to get to the police. . . ."

"It won't be necessary now," Joe replied. "When I returned, there was no sign of them."

"Well, that may resolve the immediate problem," I pointed out, "but they will be back, as ugly and violent as ever. I don't want to reopen the restaurant, Joe. Those drunken animals are too wild and unpredictable. I listened to their ravings tonight and it wasn't only food and vodka they wanted. They were asking for women. I won't subject my child and myself to that. If we were ever to fall into their hands, we would both be ruined for life."

Joe did not dispute my decision, because by now it was obvious that my heart and mind had long since crossed the ocean. I no longer identified with this place, no longer thought of it as anything but somewhere from which to escape.

But before that was to be, a new obsession took control of my life. I learned of the whereabouts of Joseph Szalai, the police commissioner who only a year ago had allowed the Hungarian Zandars to verbally and physically abuse me as he stood by in silence, no longer caring to remember that he had once been given credit at our store, or that we had always treated him as a friend. I recalled the insults and bruises I had received at his bidding and advised Magda that here was a score that would have to be settled before we made our way to America.

With my niece, Olga, I journeyed to the little town of Kis Varda, deep in the motherland of Hungary, where Joseph Szalai now lived. We went directly to the Hungarian Police to report the cruelties he had perpetrated upon the Jews during the Nazi occupation.

"In addition to these crimes," I said, "I have it on the best authority that Joseph Szalai is currently in the possession of many valuable items which were stolen from Jewish families in and around Kralovo Nad Tisza. I believe if you search his house, you will find these items, and I and many others will readily attest to his brutality against our people."

The Hungarian police did not hesitate to process the search warrant needed to investigate the Szalai home. When we first arrived at his residence, we were met by his wife, who quickly came out of the house and greeted us in the yard.

"Mrs. Weisberger, how good to see you again!" she remarked warmly, as if the past activities of her husband were now little more than ancient history. She, like all too many others, seemed to believe that the end of the war had somehow wiped their slate clean.

I returned her greeting with a curt nod, not trusting myself to offer any reply. I knew the police had better control of their emotions, and so could act more efficiently than I.

"And what brings you gentlemen out here today?" she asked cordially. I studied her face closely as the police told her they had a warrant to search her house.

"Oh, but this isn't my house," she said with a shrewdness I hadn't thought her capable of. "This is the home of my parents. I live in Anarcs with my husband, Joseph."

"And where is your husband now?" one of the officers asked then.

"In Anarcs," she replied calmly.

As we left to make our way there, the police paused long enough to instruct the local post office officials that they were to deny Mrs. Szalai the use of the public telephone. Even so, she somehow managed to contact her husband, who was not altogether unprepared for our arrival.

Szalai had taken a job in a Jewish brewery, seeming to feel that this would not only speak well for him, but also place him above suspicion.

The police asked that he be brought to us. When he entered the room where we were waiting, he paled at the very sight of me.

"Do you know these ladies?" one of the Hungarian officers asked him abruptly.

"W-Why yes . . . yes, of course! Mrs. Weisberger and Olga. How good to see you dear ladies again."

"Never mind that," the officer snapped. "Just answer the questions. Where do you know these women from?"

"Oh, but I'm sure they must have told you. I was once police commissioner of the little village now known as Kiralyhäza, where we all lived."

"And exactly what acts of cruelty did these people suffer at your hands during the Nazi occupation?"

"Why, I really don't know what you mean."

"Very well. Come along."

He was dragged from the brewery sputtering and protesting and, after we had all returned to his house, it was thoroughly searched. It did not yield as much as I had hoped, but the evidence was damaging enough. Olga recognized a dress in the closet that had belonged to her mother along with several blouses and one of her own skirts.

"These shirts belonged to my father and brothers," she said, as she pointed an accusing finger at

Joseph Szalai. "Why, even those trousers he is wearing are not his own."

We found beautifully monogrammed bedding that had once belonged to the Schreibers, an affluent family who never returned after the war.

While Szalai continued to deny his part in any criminal activities against the Jews, one of the Hungarian officers overturned the mattress on his bed and found several guns and his uniform with the Nazi emblems still on it. He had also saved the medals he had received for terrorizing the community. As he stood there, trembling and wringing his hands, I made no attempt to disguise my pleasure. The material things did not interest me as much as having Szalai in police custody. At last he would receive a taste of his own medicine. To me, it was a dream come true!

The police confiscated everything they found and then arrested Szalai. We knew he would be interrogated throughout the balance of that day, and so returned the following morning to police headquarters to see what they had learned.

"We questioned him for half the night, but could not get him to admit anything," one of the Hungarians told us. "He denies every act of which he has been accused. Would you care to see him now?"

"Indeed I would!" I said. "Let him deny his crimes to my face, if he can."

When Szalai was brought before me, I saw that his face was black and blue and severely swollen.

"How does it feel?" I asked him in a contemptuous tone. "It is not quite so pleasurable, is it, when you are on the wrong end of the stick?"

"Do you still deny that you are responsible for cruel and inhuman acts against this woman and her family?" the officer pressed again.

"Y-Yes! Yes, I deny everything!" Szalai wailed. "Mrs. Weisberger, why are you doing this?"

"Keep still!" the officer commanded. "What did you do in the Ghetto?"

"I don't know what you mean! I've told you everything I know," Szalai insisted.

"What have you done with all the valuables you stole from the homes of those who were taken away by the Nazis?"

"You already have everything! There is nothing more. You have taken all that I own!"

"The question of ownership has not yet been firmly established, but it appears altogether doubtful that you are the rightful owner of any of your possessions."

"I am not a thief!" Szalai shouted angrily. "I am not a cruel and sadistic man as these women would have you believe! During the war I followed orders. I did my job. I—"

The police officer silenced him with a sharp kick and, as Szalai cowered in a corner of the room, the Hungarians sneered at his timid behavior.

"You would not know it to look at him now," I told them, "but there was a time when he behaved like a tyrant, when everybody trembled at the very thought of what he was capable of."

"Those times are past," Szalai's interrogator assured me. "Now, he is a rat caught in his own trap. You have nothing more to fear from the likes of him."

After another hour of relentless questioning, Szalai was returned to his cell and, later that day, we returned to the house that Mrs. Szalai had insisted belonged to her parents. Armed with another search warrant, we entered these premises and looked about to see what we could find.

We discovered some beautiful furniture that had once belonged to Dr. Sternberg, the physician in our town, and some lovely Persian rugs. After these and many other things were confiscated, we discussed the matter of Szalai himself.

"His sentence depends in large measure on your ability to bring forth non-Jewish witnesses to his war crimes," we were told. I promised to do everything I could.

Once we had returned home, I went to visit the mayor of the neighboring village of Charna, and asked what he remembered of Police Commissioner Joseph Szalai.

"Remember him? I remember him only too well," the mayor replied in a cryptic tone. "Why do you ask?"

I explained that I had been instrumental in having Szalai arrested and that I needed witnesses to appear at his trial.

"I will be pleased to testify against him," the

mayor assured me. "Furthermore, I can give you the names of many others who will also be happy to cooperate."

This was a bit of luck I hadn't counted on, and following every lead, I soon returned to the Police Department of Kis Varda with a long list of people willing to testify against Szalai.

Some six weeks later, I received a subpoena to appear at the trial. Soon afterward, Szalai's brother came to the neighboring village of Charna, where the witnesses had been assembled, for the express purpose of buying their silence. But no one was willing to be bribed—except the mayor. While this seemed somewhat ironic in itself, there was a greater irony to follow.

The witnesses all traveled by train to appear at Szalai's trial, and while the trip was under way, the mayor discovered his pocket watch had been stolen. He did not hesitate to bring this to the attention of Szalai's brother, insisting that he should be reimbursed for its full value. The brother did not see this as any responsibility of his and, when he refused to pay, the mayor threatened to expose his bribery activities. Although this was not the wisest thing for him to do, he did not hesitate to carry out his threat and, as a result, promptly lost his position as mayor.

For me, the trial had been a long anticipated event, but even as the hour drew near, I began to hear rumors that the Russians were planning to close down the border where we lived. As quickly as I could, I sent Magda and Olga to Prague, via Budapest, and began making hasty preparations for my own escape. But even with so much else to think about, I could not stop thinking about the trial. More than anything, I had wanted to see that man receive a harsh sentence for the things he had done. Now I realized I would probably never know the outcome.

In early December 1945, I devised a plan for crossing the border which involved paying 2,000 pengos to a railroad engineer for transporting me in a freight train. This train made weekly journeys into Katovice for coal. While I was allowed to travel in an open car for a time, as we neared the border, the engineer ordered me into a coal bin which was little more than a small hole under the floor of the locomotive.

I glanced at him in disbelief when he indicated I should crawl into this tiny space, for I hardly saw how it could be managed.

"You will be cramped, but if you value your life, you will manage it," he said calmly. Since there was little time for argument, I did as I was told.

We reached the border around eight o'clock in the morning. The Russian border patrol came aboard, searching for contraband and anyone who might be attempting to cross the border illegally. Suddenly, the very small space in which I was hidden did not seem nearly small enough. Hearing voices and heavy footsteps on every side, I felt certain I would soon be found. But the engineer acted quickly when he chose, and this time he made the train belch such huge clouds of smoke that it was difficult for the Russians to see. An unfortunate side effect of this clever smoke screen was the smoke itself, since my tiny compartment soon became a suffocating enclosure, one that was no less threatening to my survival than the Russians themselves. To me, it now seemed only a matter of choosing one form of death over another. My lungs were seared with every intake of that hot steam, although I dared not gasp or cough for fear of calling attention to myself.

At long last the train began moving again, and now I could only anxiously await the moment of my release. But time went on, and the train continued on its path, either because the engineer did not feel we had reached a point of safety, or—*oh, horrible thought*—because he had forgotten about me! The longer I waited to be freed, the more claustrophobic I became. I could not move . . . I could not breathe . . . and I knew that if I were not soon released, I could not live.

Not until I had reached a state of utter hopelessness did I sense that the train was slowing and coming to a stop. When at last the door to my tiny compartment was opened, I peered outside and then felt the steadying hand of the railroad engineer on my arm. As he gently pulled me forward, I rolled out onto the ground in a cramped little ball, unable to straighten my limbs or to stand on my own. My clothes were soaked through from the damp steam, and I felt as pathetic and bedraggled as a mongrel in the rain.

"Here, let me help you up," the engineer said. "You may ride with me in the locomotive and dry out your things. No one will harm you now."

"Where are we?" I asked curiously, and was told that we were on our way to Zolna.

Immediately, my spirits greatly improved, since I knew that once there, I would be able to change into fresh clothing and then catch an express train to Prague. My daughter and Olga would be waiting and, very soon now, this nightmare would be over.

9

The reunion in Prague was as joyous and emotional as I had imagined it would be. As we embraced one another at the Wilson Station, I blessed our good fortune in being together once more.

"We have known some dreadful times," I said to Magda, "but much good luck as well. You will not believe my journey in the coal bin of that train. I have so much to tell you, I hardly know where to begin."

Later, after we had settled ourselves into a rented hotel apartment, we began to work on re-establishing our citizenship and also applied for passports.

The Czechoslovakians greeted us with open arms, which was strange but wonderful after our exposure to the Russians. It reinforced my feelings that we would never live under any government as oppressively restrictive as Communism. Many Russian Jewish soldiers had advised us to go to the West, saying that this was what they themselves would have done had they not had families in Russia. After a taste of Western life, they had all grown averse to the Communist ways, although they remained hopelessly resigned to them.

Throughout the war, their level of poverty had sparked an unusual quality of greed. It was not uncommon to see Russian soldiers sporting several wristwatches on their arms, and in one case, I saw a soldier with watches running from the wrists to the elbows in the most garish display of looter's bounty I had ever seen. I watched him hold the watches to his ear, then shake his head and curse. It all struck me as highly curiously behavior until I realized that many of the Russians did not know enough to wind the watches. When they stopped ticking, they thought the watches were broken, and so the next logical step for them was to simply get another watch.

I thought about these and other things as I waited for the necessary documents to reinstate our citizenship. The waiting was difficult but, in the interim, Olga met and married a fine gentleman by the name of Bela Vilkovitz who had lost a wife and two sons in Auschwitz. I was more than happy to attend to the wedding preparations, because I was extremely fond of Olga and overjoyed that a new way of life had at last opened up for her.

It was a happy, festive time for us and we allowed ourselves to enjoy this special day with carefree abandon.

Eventually, Olga and her new husband would find their way to New York, where they would establish a grocery business and welcome the birth of a beautiful little daughter, Naomi. Naomi would later earn a degree in psychiatry and, although her father would not live to see this day, Olga and her child would remain close, even after Naomi had married and started a family of her own.

Olga's wedding momentarily took my mind away from all the paperwork needed to bring us to America. Once the festivities were over, however, I began to fret that our immigration might never be accomplished. At every turn, we were subjected to greater confusion and seemingly endless delays. On January 2, 1946, this dream finally became a reality and, while it put us all in a highly festive mood, we were totally without means to celebrate. Both money and food were in short supply and, had my sister Pearl in Philadelphia not been in a position to sustain us, we could no longer have managed on our own.

When at last our affidavits to immigrate arrived, I immediately took them to the American Consulate and applied for a visa. After that, there was nothing to do but wait, a way of life I had lost all patience with. The apartment was costing 100 kronas per day, a sizable sum in those days. Since I knew we could not afford it indefinitely, I was eager to be on my way. Every delay generated the start of some new anxiety, and not without good reason. One day, I learned through the newspapers that the Russians were demanding that all people born in Pod Karpatska Rus (also known as Ruthenia) be returned to their birthplace. We were told we would have to register at Russian Headquarters but, since we had no desire to go back, we simply ignored this order. Others reacted in much the same manner, some choosing to go on to Germany where they were detained in displaced persons camps for a number of years. Those who entered Palestine illegally continued to live like escaped convicts. After everything they had already been through, they were still without a home.

Even with my Czechoslovakian citizenship reinstated, I remained ill-at-ease each time deportation of the Ruthanians became newsworthy. When I learned that transports had been organized to return these people to their homeland, I refused any longer to venture out into the streets. I wrote a letter—clearly edged in panic—to my sister advising her of my fear that time was running out for us.

A few weeks later, at a time when it seemed to me that nothing good could ever happen again, we received two plane tickets to New York, via Paris, France. At this point, I went back to the consulate and asked what could be done to expedite our visa before the Russians somehow succeeded in deporting us.

"I can certainly understand your feelings of urgency in this matter," I was told, "but nothing more can be done until your turn comes up. It is quite possible that your visa is already being processed and that you will receive it shortly from Washington, D.C. All requests for visas are handled in the order in which they are received. It is a slow but systematic process—and of course, the only fair one."

At this juncture, I was no longer able to decide what was fair or unfair. I returned to our room and told the girls what had transpired. "They make this long speech about wishing to assist you in every way, but it all comes back to waiting and more waiting. It isn't their neck, so what do they care?"

On May 16, 1946, we finally received the visas, but our airline tickets from Paris to New York had been scheduled for departure on May 10. Anticipating that something like this might happen, I had already contacted Paris by wire to reschedule our flight for a later date. When at last the confirmation for an alternate flight arrived, I was appalled to see that our departure was now scheduled for July 18.

Oh God, how are we expected to sustain ourselves for another two months? I thought, knowing our reserves of money and food were extremely low.

Still, we somehow managed the unmanageable, and then traveled to Paris by train, in time to spend the night in a hotel on July 17. The next morning, I was informed by the airlines that our flight had been delayed for twenty-four hours, but decided to accept this in good spirits and devote the extra day to a bit of sightseeing. In recent days it had occurred to me that my intense behavior over anything and everything that happened would appear extremely strange to those who did not remember me this way. For their sakes, if not my own, I would have to make some attempt to react normally to life's little adversities so that I might be properly received and accepted by those who had not known the horrors we had left behind.

Still, my resolution to relax was short-lived. The following day, I learned there were no available seats on our rescheduled flight.

The clerk at the airline office was taken aback at the angry tirade I directed at him, although I felt totally justified in my fury.

"I am tired of being made a fool of!" I shouted at him, as others turned and watched. "At every turn I am told that I have confirmed reservations which are later canceled and rescheduled according to your latest whim. My funds are limited, and I cannot continue to stay on here. I was promised a flight to New York on July 18 and, if it is to be changed again, then this had better be the final change!"

"You are right, of course," the clerk kept mumbling nervously. "You may count on seats on our TWA flight which leaves during the late afternoon on July 20. I'll take personal responsibility for your departure at that time."

It all seemed like just so many empty words but, when at last the day arrived, we boarded the plane for New York. I still believed someone might come along at the last minute and eject us from our seats, but the flight took off without incident. Once I saw the soft bed of clouds stretching out beneath us as far as we could see, I knew nothing more could keep us from our ultimate destination.

I have always remembered it as a pleasant flight, although it would be considered extremely tedious by today's standards. The TWA propeller aircraft landed twice along its way for refueling: once at the Shannon Airport in Ireland, and again in Newfoundland. In Newfoundland, a humorous incident occurred, although it was somewhat unnerving at the time. At the airport restaurant, we were served fresh grapefruit halves, something totally new to us. Since we hadn't any idea how to eat them, we looked to see how the other passengers were dealing with this succulent food. Once we had mastered the art of eating grapefruit, we discovered that this fruit had a truly delectable taste. It turned out to be one of the few things Magda managed to eat because she had found it virtually impossible to keep any food on her stomach throughout the flight.

The entire flight from Paris to New York took

twenty-four hours and, when at last I saw we were approaching American soil, my heart began to pound crazily. It occurred to me I might not recognize anyone who would be waiting for us, since my last recollection of my sisters went back to girlhood days. We had all changed considerably through the years, but none more drastically than I. Once again, I became painfully aware of my appearance and wished I looked healthier and more wholesome.

Although I had heard stories of people kissing the ground when they first arrived in this new land, I had always wondered if these tales weren't slightly exaggerated. And yet, when the plane landed, this was my first impulse—an impulse I eagerly obeyed. It did not concern me what others might think. Anyone who could not understand such an emotional gesture could also never conceive of the loss of personal freedom and what it could mean to finally regain it.

We moved quickly through Customs and, as we did, I saw that someone seemed to be waving in our direction. As I looked more closely, I knew beyond any shadow of a doubt that this was my sister Pearl. Now the processing line became suddenly sluggish and interminably long. Fighting the urge to push everyone else aside, I kept my eyes riveted on her and thought how little she had changed, even after fifteen years. Once I had been cleared to do so, I rushed toward her and everything that had once been good about my life.

We held each other and laughed and cried, which brought to mind many happy childhood experiences and the realization that we still had roots. Even after all this, the permanence and stability of family roots had miraculously survived; they had been torn and ravaged but not destroyed. What was left would be enough to build upon.

I had imagined all the things I would say at the time of this happy reunion, but now there seemed nothing to say. My sister's husband, Louis, and son, Paul, had remained at a respectful distance while Pearl and I greeted one another, but now moved forward to guide us through the terminal. As we walked to the car, the conversation continued to buzz around me, but even throughout the drive home, I could think of nothing to say. Instead, I stared out the window and watched the streets of Philadelphia move past like a lovely mural, too wonderful to be believed. Here there were no barracks, no guards, no barbed wire fences, no mud or odor of burning flesh. Here it was possible to walk the streets without fear of being captured . . . or deported . . . or killed. Here there was safety and a quality of life long since forgotten. Decent food and housing, well-manicured lawns, peaceful streets and friendly neighbors. A chance to grow and prosper and to be whatever one chose to be without restraints or threats of reprisal. It could not all be absorbed in a single day, and perhaps not for a long time to come. To casually accept so many wondrous things, so many marvelous opportunities was beyond my comprehension. To be surrounded by so many personal privileges and freedoms was almost beyond belief.

Once inside my sister's home, I felt compelled to explore every room, to take note of stylish and modern furnishings and accessories that worked well together and complimented the exemplary taste of their owners.

Having scavenged for everything we needed to equip the restaurant, the bar and our simple living quarters, I had grown accustomed to living amid a hodgepodge of mismatched items. It had not seemed particularly important at the time, but now I realized what a truly pathetic way of life it had been.

That night, we slept in a lovely guest room with fine linens on the bed and awoke the next morning to our first day in a new country.

I eagerly raced down the stairs to find my sister already on the phone, calling everyone she knew to tell them of our arrival. Over breakfast, I watched her dial one number after the other and thought what a wonderful thing it was to have this device right here in the house. In the old country, we had had to share a single public telephone, which was somewhat unpleasant during inclement weather, but still better than no telephone at all.

My sister's calls resulted in a seemingly endless stream of friends and relatives to the house. Once they had confirmed that we had truly survived, they asked for any information we could give them about their own loved ones who had not returned.

We did the best we could, trying to remember all the familiar faces we had seen in the camps and after our liberation, but what we were able to tell them was of small consolation. It was difficult to explain the mass confusion we had been forced to live in, or how quickly people became separated because of the constant shifting about.

But still the questions came, and then one day a newscaster arrived representing one of the local radio stations. He asked if we would grant him an interview. When he asked that I relate everything I had seen and experienced in the concentration camp, however, I quickly declined.

"But it is of great historical importance," he insisted, "something we must let the rest of the world know about! And the truth can only be known if we are able to gain the cooperation of those who were directly involved."

"I can appreciate that," I said tiredly, "but I think your request is a trifle premature. Those who were there and survived the atrocities of the Nazi regime have no immediate desire to relive those experiences through public interviews and other forms of publicity. I doubt you will find many who are up to that. In time, the telling may become easier, but for now, it is simply impossible."

When the newscaster continued to persist, Magda stepped between us and politely but firmly ushered him to the door. I found his persistent questioning had totally exhausted me, perhaps because it reminded me of so many earlier interrogations, and I quietly excused myself and went upstairs to rest.

In time, we started visiting people outside the house and were relieved to find everyone extremely hospitable and exceptionally kind. Their questions were few and carefully worded. For the most part, they seemed more interested in our welfare and how they might help us make a successful adjustment to this new land.

As old fears and apprehensions began to fall away, I became more outgoing and friendly, although I was unable to keep from dwelling on certain aspects of the old life. One particular question that kept returning to mind was the fate of Joseph Szalai. I had tried to convince myself that what became of him no longer mattered, but my taste for revenge refused to die. I wanted to know that this man had received the most severe punishment possible.

One evening, I wrote a letter to the Police Headquarters in Kis Varda requesting that they let me know the outcome of the trial. I enclosed a self-addressed envelope to expedite the earliest reply.

Soon afterward, the answer came and I was advised of the following:

October 8, 1946

Dear Madam Weisberger—

On the 18th of August, this year, I received your letter in which you enquire about Joszef Szalai who was a Police Chief in the past. The aforementioned trial is still in process. He is still incarcerated while judgment is being deliberated. I am not at liberty to give you all the information, but I can tell you this, that everyone who committed a crime will get just punishment. Please have faith in the present Police Department and judges for they fulfill their duties very conscientiously.

Yours truly,

Klar Miksa, Lieutenant
Chief of Police, Kis Varda

It was the last that I would ever learn of Joseph Szalai and, while this lack of information would continue to disturb me, there were other matters that took immediate precedence.

I had been receiving regular correspondence from a fine gentleman named Menhard Lebovitz, who had once lived in the same Czechoslovakian village where we had resided. I remembered him as a very fine tailor who catered to the nobility in town and who regularly employed a staff of ten to twelve people. Before the war, he had been considered quite well-to-do, but the war had cost him everything, including twenty-six members of his family.

After I returned to our village, I learned that he too had survived and that he shared my dream to go to America.

"It would please me greatly if you would care to combine our dreams and travel to America as my wife," he said to me one evening. While I clearly heard the words, I continued to question his motives. It seemed to me that this proposal might be nothing more than the product of loneliness and, were I to accept, it could be a sign of the same thing.

I could not trust my feelings so soon after the war. It seemed it would be quite easy to do all the right things for all the wrong reasons, and so I dared not succumb to impulse. I gave no further thought to Menhard Lebovitz's proposal, and eventually he left Czechoslovakia, arriving in America one month earlier than I.

Since my sister Pearl had advised him, along with so many others, that I would be staying with her, I arrived at her home only to find a letter from Menhard Lebovitz waiting for me. I considered it in the light of a thoughtful gesture and would have dismissed it at that, except that his letters continued. Suddenly, the question of marriage was reopened.

At that time, he was staying in the home of his

married sister, Tillie Marton, who resided in Chicago. My older sister, Sarah, who had come to America when I was only five years old, also lived in Chicago. It was inevitable I would spend some time with her and, after two months in Philadelphia, I was finally ready to make the trip. Magda came too.

Sarah and her daughter, Lillian, lived in a one bedroom apartment on Troy Street. After Magda and I arrived, there were four occupants in that tiny place, but our great joy in being reunited overshadowed every inconvenience. Still, it was not an easy life. We did not speak English and needed jobs desperately. With Sarah's help and influence, we were finally taken on at an electronics plant, where we were put to work assembling cables.

I found the work extremely pleasant, despite the language barrier. My daughter and I worked diligently, for we had a long way to go in the course of rebuilding our lives. Having arrived in this country with only the clothes on our backs, we were grateful for any employment opportunity and applied ourselves to every task with great drive and determination.

Since we were all now in Chicago, I realized that a visit from Menhard Lebovitz was inevitable. When at last he came to call, I found him to be even more vocally persuasive than he had been in his letters. As I listened to him talk, the idea of marriage became a more plausible idea. There was a critical housing shortage in Chicago in 1946, however, making such plans a trifle unrealistic.

"Even if we *were* to get married," I suggested at one point, "there are simply no living quarters available. I have already checked into that because we are all so crowded in Sarah's little apartment, and by now I had hoped to put an end to that."

Menhard Lebovitz refused to be discouraged. Since I had said enough to let him know I had actually considered the idea of marrying him, he reacted as if the matter were already settled.

"You will stay on with Sarah, and I will stay on with Tillie until we can find a place," he said with an air of great assurance. "Things will work out for us, Shari. We are entitled to some happiness now."

After he left, I watched his retreating figure and felt my eyes fill with tears. The war had cost him a wife and two sons, and the pain of this loss was permanently etched into his face. His stooped shoulders seemed to have carried the weight of the world, and he was given to periodic fits of melancholy which he sought to avoid by speaking with gentle persuasion of building a new life. I knew he was right, that we would have to look forward in order to keep from being overpowered by the past. In his quiet, almost humble way, he was fighting for a reason to go on, and I could only feel privileged that he had chosen me to be that reason.

On December 10, 1946, we were married in

Chicago. We went to live in the apartment of an elderly woman who had advertised an extra room for rent. When her landlord discovered what she had done, he threatened to evict her unless she ordered us to move. Reluctantly she did so and, as she struggled through this dreadful piece of news, I could only wonder what would become of us now.

In the end, we went back to live with my husband's sister, where we stayed for six months until we were able to locate a basement apartment. Although it was a very modest dwelling, with exposed pipes running along the ceiling and a liberal infestation of water bugs, I was convinced it was quite the most wonderful place in the world.

"At last we are on our own, Manny! Truly independent. I cannot believe our good fortune!" I said happily.

"I am glad you are so easy to please," my husband responded with a cynical smile. "All I see is a greasy oven and a cockroach in every corner."

"Leave that to me," I said enthusiastically. "I will get some poison to get rid of the bugs, and I'll scrub this place until it sparkles."

My husband was no less determined to make a good life and worked first one and then two jobs to bring in extra income. After dinner, he would report to a clothing store where he did alteration work. Since we saved every dollar we could, we were soon able to buy a small cleaning and tailoring business.

Although we did not speak the language, we managed to communicate effectively through the quality of our work, and so built a nice clientele.

We worked side by side until I discovered that I was pregnant; the pregnancy was a difficult one and gave rise to some old gallbladder problems. My condition was further complicated by my age. When my son Sheldon was born in May 1948, I was forty years old, the oldest mother in the maternity ward at the Edgewater Hospital in Chicago.

But every problem and complication was quickly forgotten with the arrival of this beautiful baby boy. He was truly a blessing in our lives, sparking a new ray of sunshine in the heart of my husband, who had lost the sons of his previous marriage.

During the time of my confinement, Magda began working in the store and quickly became a competent assistant to my hard-working husband. The business prospered, and life was good.

By now, Magda had blossomed into a lovely twenty-year-old woman who dated occasionally but without any serious involvements.

And then one day, we attended a wedding in the Lebovitz family where one of the Lebovitz women took particular notice of her. Later, this woman would tell her son, Ernie: "I met this lovely and thoroughly charming girl today. I want you to call her for a date."

The boy, Ernest Willinger, was not pleased with his mother's attempts at matchmaking. He had been on his own since the age of nineteen and now was an independent, strong-willed fellow of twenty-six years.

"I assure you, this girl is different," his mother insisted, which made Ernie even more certain her choice would not appeal to him.

"It's totally pointless," he told her. "You know we never agree on these things."

"But this time you will see I am right," his mother insisted, not once but many times, until at last her son knew there was no way to put an end to her pressure except to invite Magda to go out with him.

"Once I've done as you've asked, Mama, you must promise you will never bother me about this matter again," Ernie said, and his mother quickly agreed.

Soon afterward, Ernest Willinger arrived at the tailor shop of Menhard Lebovitz. He evaluated the girl from every angle before admitting to her he was not a customer. When he finally introduced himself and invited her out, Magda shyly accepted. A month later, they were engaged to be married.

Magda and Ernie were married when Sheldon was only five weeks old. They lived with us until they were able to locate an apartment of their own. Eventually, Ernie established himself in the field of venetian blind manufacturing, and I was pleased to see how hard-working and industrious he was.

It was during this period that Magda was plagued with a constantly recurring nightmare, one that even the security of marriage and the comfort of family could not prevent. Her hysterical screams would awaken the entire household. After she had managed to calm herself, she would relate the dream to me in all its vivid detail.

"I am still a child in the dream, playing with some friends. My sisters, Veronica and Lillian, are playing close by. It is a warm, pleasant day. We are all so happy together. And then suddenly this big black beast comes into the scene. He is galloping toward us at a furious speed. There isn't time to move or even to cry out. I sit and watch as he approaches, seeing now that he is a black bull of truly gigantic proportions. He seems to be snorting fire and has wild, gleaming eyes. As he descends upon us, there isn't time to run. He rushes past me and crushes and kills my younger sisters. I am totally helpless, paralyzed with fear, and can only sit there and watch."

Generally, the dream would end there, but it was no less vivid to me than it was to Magda. Symbolically, I knew the bull represented the Nazi war machine that had torn the younger girls away from us quickly and ruthlessly. Yes, they had been crushed and killed by a big, ugly beast; in that sense the dream was altogether accurate.

A year and a half later, Magda's first daughter,

Judith, was born, and after that there were no more nocturnal visits from the huge, raging bull. With the birth of Judith, my small son, Sheldon, became an uncle.

We took great pride in watching these beautiful children grow and, by the time my son was of school age, he was quite impressed with the idea of being an uncle. He was also an excellent student and decided at a very early age that he wished to become a doctor. Knowing it was not uncommon for children to change their minds about such things, we were not inclined to take him seriously, but he went on to fulfill this dream.

Meanwhile, Magda and Ernie's family expanded to include a second daughter, Donne. I thoroughly enjoyed my role as a grandparent and was deeply saddened when I learned of their decision to move to Arizona. But they had not been having an easy time of it. Ernie was forced to close the business and look for other means to support his family when venetian blinds went out of style. At this time, it was not uncommon for them to subsist on fifteen dollars a week, which was hardly adequate for a family of that size. Through a brother-in-law in Skokie, Illinois, Ernie eventually became involved in rototilling and landscape contracting, which would serve him in good stead once they settled in Arizona.

The year was 1958 and our tailoring business in Chicago's north side had grown and flourished. Although I felt the urge to follow Magda wherever she went, I knew better than to suggest such a thing to Manny. He had worked long and hard to establish what he had in the business and it would have been altogether unreasonable to ask him to walk away from it. So, I visited Magda and her family in the summer and told myself the visit was enough, although the thought persisted that we would be much happier in this warm, sunny climate.

In subtle yet persistent ways, I began to enumerate the advantages of moving west, stressing that the Eastern winters were becoming more severe, and that there was an easier, more carefree life waiting for us.

My suggestions were labelled preposterous, as I had known they would be, but I refused to be discouraged.

I knew by now that Manny could not be coerced, only convinced, and over a long period of time, I managed to accomplish this. When Sheldon graduated from high school, we sold our ranch-style home in Evanston, Illinois, and headed to Arizona.

On July 25, 1967, we arrived in Arizona and moved into a lovely apartment Magda had rented for us. Almost immediately, Manny began to fret about being unemployed, although we had sold the business for a nice profit, and he very much needed a rest.

"There is no time to rest," he insisted, with an edge of impatience in his voice. "I must decide what I am to do. This is a totally different lifestyle here. People dress so casually! All I have seen is play clothes and blue jeans. There may not even be a market for fine tailoring. I must find out, because that is the only thing I know."

In the month of October, Manny secured a tailoring job in a small downtown establishment. The salary was ridiculously low, but it gave him something to do while I looked about for a business to buy. I was frustrated by the outrageously high prices for what was being offered. The locations were poor, the clientele more spasmodic than loyal, and most of these businesses had been poorly managed, which meant that much would have to be done—and undone—before they could show a reasonable profit.

At long last, I had had my fill of it. "Why should we buy someone else's headaches?" I asked Manny one evening. "We can start our own business. There are a number of shopping centers here, any one of which would provide an excellent location."

"At an exorbitant price!" Manny quickly countered. "We had better think about moving into a converted house and settling for a cheaper neighborhood."

But I knew that the outward appearance of the store had an aesthetic value that could not be underestimated. I continued to look at shopping center facilities and finally found a store in a center that was still under construction. Since the management was eager to draw new tenants, we were able to acquire this space for an extremely reasonable rental, and soon afterward opened Manny's Custom Tailoring.

Meanwhile, Sheldon entered Arizona State University, and later went on to complete his education at the Philadelphia College of Osteopathic Medicine. He eventually married a lovely girl, Robyn Schwartz, and established residency in Berwyn, Pennsylvania, as a General Practitioner. Sheldon and Robyn blessed us with two additional grandsons, Benjamin and Michael.

By now, Magda's husband, Ernie, had become a highly respected businessman, enabling him to provide a secure and comfortable life for his family.

In 1977, Manny and I sold our business and retired, then returned to Pennsylvania to visit with our son and his family. On the way back, we stopped in Chicago to see my sister Sarah, and my nephew, Joseph Kraus, who had come to the United States shortly after we had. We reminisced about past experiences, both good and bad, agreeing that we all had much to be thankful for.

Manny and I were planning a trip to Israel in October and could think of very little else as the time drew near. But in July, my beloved husband was stricken with a heart attack which took him from me at the age of 74. Our passports for Israel arrived the day after Manny passed away.

It seemed like another cruel irony of life but, while I felt a tremendous sadness, I could no longer feel bitterness. The bitterness had gone with the years, replaced by a gratitude for those good things that had somehow evolved out of so many dreadful experiences. The greatest gift of all had been the gift of survival, for it brought with it the knowledge that life itself is a precious miracle.

Some thirty years after the war, Magda and Ernest Willinger traveled to Israel to attend the wedding of a member of Ernie's family. The wedding was a large and elegant affair, attended by approximately 250 people, who were seated in small groups at individual tables.

During the festivities, Ernie's aunt suddenly approached in the company of a young girl who immediately captured Magda's attention. Intrigued by the intensity of Magda's concentration, Ernie carefully studied his wife as Magda continued to study the young girl. Normally calm and poised, Magda's eyes grew huge and round, and her manner became increasingly excitable as she grabbed the young woman's arm and demanded to know her name.

The woman responded by giving her married name, which was Yaari.

Although this was not familiar to her, Magda continued to stare at the girl, determined to make some elusive yet vital connection. Then, as the young girl attempted to move away, Magda once again grabbed her arm, refusing to let go.

"And just who are *you*?" the girl finally demanded, having become suddenly impatient with Magda's relentless interrogation.

"My name is Magda Weisberger," Magda said, sensing that her maiden name would have some significant impact upon this young woman.

Immediately, the young woman's countenance changed. "Magda!" she cried. "It's Terri! My sister Irene and I were in the concentration camp with you. Oh God, had it not been for your angel mother, we would never have survived!"

At that, the two women embraced and, totally overcome by emotion, began to laugh and cry, as others curiously looked on.

As they compared notes, Magda learned that Terri Yaari was happily married and living in Ramat Gan, near Tel Aviv. Her sister's married name was Epstein and she had gone to live in a *moshav,* a cooperative commune.

Magda's ability to recognize Terri after so many years was later attributed to her incredible memory for faces, particularly *this* face, with its naturally pale complexion which, in the camp, had literally been ashen because of her extremely emaciated state.

But even more remarkable than Magda's ability to recognize this friend was the reason for Terri's attendance at the wedding. Terri was herself a Willinger and, in fact, Ernie's second cousin, something Ernie and Magda would never have known had this sudden and totally unexpected reunion not taken place.

After the wedding, Magda and Terri established a regular correspondence which continues to this day. Founded in an atmosphere that neither woman expected to survive, their friendship has endured—even as they have.

Coming very close to death is the best way to learn what life is all about—and perhaps the only way to truly understand its value.

Each day has a purpose, although that purpose is not always clear, and it is important to look forward with optimism and joy.

Since we were unable to avoid the atrocities of a world gone mad, we chose to take pride in having endured and survived.

Those who were lost to us, we will meet in Heaven. That will be the last and the finest reunion of all.

EPILOGUE

Two generations passed before I returned to Europe in 1985. I had decided to go on a group tour of Austria, Switzerland and Germany with hopes of finally finding the grave of my husband and Magda's father, Solomon Weisberger.

For forty years, the words of Sam Farkas, the friend and neighbor who had had the unpleasant task of telling me that Solomon would never return, echoed in my mind:

> I spent many hours with your husband. In our conversations, he shared his feelings and fears. 'I have no one to live for,' he told me. 'My wife, Shari, had a baby, and we both know that mothers and babies were sent straight to the gas chambers. My two-year-old Lillian, my seven-year-old Veronica, surely they had no chance. My oldest daughter, Magda, was

a frail girl of fifteen who was not capable of the hard labor Germany needed. As you can see, they all have perished,' Solomon Weisberger told me.

We did not leave together. . . . I was liberated with your husband and remained with him throughout the typhoid siege. . . . We were placed in a makeshift hospital in Wels, Austria. . . . We did not leave together. . . . Your husband succumbed to the disease. I personally witnessed his death in the hospital.

It was those words that had made me realize that Solomon had given up hope because he believed he had no one to go home to. Those words had also finally convinced me to leave our home forever and come to America, a decision I have never regretted.

Still, I was determined to someday return and find Solomon, who had remained in my heart and mind since the day he boarded the train for the labor camp in 1942. This European tour was my first opportunity to locate his body, but I had not anticipated the pace at which we traveled. We saw all the popular sights, but the sight I most wished to see was Solomon's final resting place. It was not until the last day, when we returned to Vienna, that I was able to pursue my quest.

It was there that I asked our tour director, a German man, for assistance. "At the end of the war I was told that my husband died in Wels, Austria,"

I said. "Would you help me find out if this is true?"

"Of course, Frau Lebovitz. I would be most glad to call," he replied, and he promptly found the phone number of Wels' only hospital.

Although I did not speak German fluently, it was not difficult to understand some of the conversation. When he hung up the phone he turned to me. "Frau Lebovitz, they do have records of Solomon Weisberger in their archives. We are to call back in two hours to give them some time to find more information."

Two hours later the tour director made another call, one that would tell me what I had waited so very long to hear. The conversation was brief, but the director took notes intently. When the call ended, he handed me a piece of paper that said, "KZ Friedhof Catholic Cemetery, Plot Number 52, Grave Number 4." After so many, many years, I was excited to receive such accurate information. "Now," I said, "I will be able to visit my husband's grave."

Although it was the last day of the tour and I was fighting a terrible cold, I still hoped to fulfill my longtime dream. I rushed to the hotel concierge desk. "How far is it to Wels?" I asked. My heart sunk when he replied, "Three hours by train." I looked out the window and saw the pouring rain that had brought on my dreadful cold, and thought about our departure the next day. I knew I would not make it to Wels on this trip, but I vowed then to return.

When I got home to Arizona, I told Magda and her husband, Ernest, of my discovery. "We will go together," I insisted. Terrorist bombing in Vienna the next year made us reconsider the trip, but we were not idle. We contacted John McCain, our senator, and the Jewish National Fund to verify Solomon's gravesite in Wels, for we hoped to have his body exhumed and shipped to Arizona for reburial.

After a year and a half of communications with the Austrian government, Senator McCain's office reported that there was a problem. Four people were buried in each of the graves in the Jewish section of KZ Friedhof Catholic Cemetery. We checked with the JNF, which confirmed the information. When we realized we would not be able to exhume Solomon's body, I made up my mind. "We must go to Austria, then," I decided. "I will not give up. My belief in my family has gotten me this far, and I will not give up, just as my family has never given up on me."

Before we could make further plans, however, the core of the Soviet Chernobyl nuclear station exploded and released radioactive material over Eastern Europe.

Finally, in 1988, Magda, Ernest and I embarked upon our pilgrimage together. After so many years of doubt, our excitement at arriving in Vienna was tempered by our anticipation as well as the painful memories reawakened by the sound of the German language being spoken around us.

The following day, we boarded the train for Wels. It was a lovely June morning, and we were dressed comfortably in suit jackets. Outside our window, the green meadows of the rolling countryside, dotted with farms, was complemented by the clear blue sky. Some two hours later, though, we arrived in Wels in a cold, pouring rain. At the railroad station, we managed to purchase a single umbrella. All three of us, shivering in our jackets, huddled beneath it. We quickly hailed a cab, which took us to the KZ Friedhof Catholic Cemetery.

There we sought out the magistrate, W.AR. Sonntagbauer, who graciously searched through reams of paper. Finally he pulled out two sheets and handed us one. The sheet listed the names, hometowns, occupations and birth and death dates of Solomon and three other men. "These are the other men who are interred with your husband," he said. Magistrate Sonntagbauer then rose, donned his coat and picked up the other piece of paper, on which we could see a map of sorts. Still huddled under our umbrella, Magda, Ernest and I followed the magistrate back out into pouring rain.

We walked along the immaculate walkways, past the manicured plots of the Catholic cemetery to a small, grassy field. A single headstone rose from the patch of green turf. Finally, the magistrate consulted the map. He then measured off distances with careful strides. After several paces, he stopped and pointed to an unmarked spot on the ground. "This is Plot Number 52, Grave Number 4, where Solomon Weisberger is buried," said Magistrate Sonntagbauer solemnly.

Despite the overwhelming significance of the moment, Ernest had the presence of mind to ask the magistrate if he would take a photograph of us in this place we had envisioned for so long. The three of us stood, our arms linked, as he snapped the picture. The magistrate then respectfully withdrew, leaving us alone.

We approached the site with heavy hearts. To memorialize a loved one in this strange, faraway place was eerie indeed. Together, we recited the Kaddish Memorial Prayer, and we wept. Even the sky overhead opened, mingling its raindrops with our salty sorrow.

We stood in the rain at least a half-hour, praying and crying together. Then I noticed a woman staring at us from a nearby apartment. I wondered what she thought as she watched us, wondered if she knew that so many men lay here as a terrible tribute to heartlessness, wondered if she felt remorse, sorrow . . . or anything at all.

Before we left Wels that day, we ordered a granite headstone from a nearby monument maker, where we were surprised and pleased to see a wide selection of Hebrew sayings and symbols.

When we arrived at the mason's, it was almost as if he had been waiting for us, and others like us, to arrive. We ordered a stone inscribed with the names, dates of birth and death of each of the

four men who lay together forever:
>Solomon Weisberger
>Imre Foldes
>Pal Radosi
>Ernö Schwartz.

We chose a Jewish star to grace the top of the gravestone. Because we lived so far away, Ernest offered to pay the masons in full. The monument makers, however, refused even a deposit. "After we erect the stone," one of them said, "we'll send you a photograph. If you are satisfied, you can then pay the bill."

The kindness shown by these people could only help mellow our long-held bitterness toward the German people. It was difficult not to harbor such feelings after living through their apparent consent and assistance in the destruction of all we had held dear, yet this trip had helped us gain a new perspective. We discovered that the people of Wels, just twenty-five miles from Hitler's birthplace, had taken it upon themselves to turn an old schoolhouse into a hospital to aid the poor men who had been released from the camps only to contract deadly typhoid. While we could never forget the cruelty we endured, this revelation helped us realize that not all Germans were bent upon the elimination of the Jews.

Nonetheless, there were 817 men buried in this one-acre plot who, aside from the single headstone placed there by a family from Canada, had lain in obscurity for forty years. Determined that this silence must be broken, we requested information on all 817 men. We have since shared the findings with many families who still search for those they will always love.

To assist that quest, the 42-page list is now available at the Yad Vashem Memorial, site of the Holocaust Memorial; the Budapest Museum; And the libraries of Temple Beth Israel and Temple Beth El in Phoenix, Arizona, and Temple Har Zion in Scottsdale, Arizona. We also shared it with the Wiesenthal Center, which documents Holocaust history. Although the KZ Friedhof Cemetery is just a few miles from the Wiesenthal Center in Vienna, the center's researchers were unaware of the site or the efforts of the people of Wels. This realization only underscored once again the extent of the conflagration, and the depth to which it has been buried.

As Sam Farkas said, not knowing is often far worse than knowing the truth. We now not only know the truth, we know it is marked with the permanence of stone.

ACKNOWLEDGMENTS

This book would not be complete without extending sincere appreciation to the many people who have encouraged us through the years.

We thank Mr. and Mrs. Ted Basch, Mrs. Mary Cornelius, Mrs. Betty Driscoll, Mr. Morris and Mrs. Thelma Feller, Mr. Norman and Mrs. Rhoda Fuchs, Mr. Ervin and Mrs. Maria Gelbron, Mr. Irvin and Mrs. Mildred Golden, Mrs. Donne Goldstein, Mrs. Mickey Hayman, Mr. Stephen and Mrs. Darlene Hayman, Mrs. Helen Jerzy, Mr. Morris Kaplan, Mrs. Charlotte Kelly, Mrs. Judy Kelly, Father Ernest Latko, Dr. Sheldon and Mrs. Robyn Lebovitz, Mr. Myron Lee, Mrs. Elsie Mandel, Pastor George Morrison, Mr. David Newberger, Mr. William and Mrs. Peggy Pierce, Mrs. Dorothy Pickelner, Dr. F. Jeffrey and Mrs. Colleen Platt, Mrs. Julia Roth, Mrs. Heddy Spitz, Governor Fife Symington and all the others who have helped this book reach the printed page.

These pages would never have been the same without the expertise of writer Greta Bishop of Goldmark 1 and publisher Mary Westheimer of Via Writing & Publishing Services. We thank them both for their heartfelt dedication.

In addition, we especially thank Senator John McCain and his staff for confirming that there are three other men buried with Solomon Weisberger in KZ Friedhof Cemetery in Wels, Austria.

Thanks, also, to W.AR. Sonntagbauer, the magistrate who so graciously helped us at KZ Friedhof Cemetery.

Finally, we gratefully acknowledge the efforts of the mayor, doctors, nurses and the entire community of Wels, who converted an old school into a makeshift hospital in order to try to save as many lives as possible. In addition, for those, like Solomon, who could not be saved, the caring community of Wels, with an open heart and a great conscience, allotted precious land for a final resting place, then kept careful records that have allowed us, after all these years, to find some peace.